ORATIO

OR - 'OUGHT - SEE - OH

REVISED SECOND EDITION

ORATIO

OR - 'OUGHT - SEE - OH

REVISED SECOND EDITION

RHYTHMS OF PRAYER
FROM THE
HEART OF THE CHURCH

DILLON E. BARKER
JIMMY MITCHELL
EDITORS

MYSTERIUM

[LOVE GOOD]

ORATIO (REVISED SECOND EDITION)

ISBN 978-0-692-89224-4

Published by Mysterium LLC
Nashville, Tennessee, U.S.A.
LoveGoodCulture.com

NIHIL OBSTAT:
Rev. Jayd D. Neely
Censor Librorum

IMPRIMATUR:
Most Rev. David R. Choby
Bishop of Nashville
May 9, 2017

For bulk orders or group rates, email info@lovegoodculture.com.
Special thanks to Jacob Green and David Lee for their contributions to this edition.

Cover art & design by Adam Lindenau
adapted from "The Angelus" by Jean-François Millet, 1857

The Tradition of the Church
proposes to the faithful certain
rhythms of praying
intended to nourish continual prayer.

Some are daily, such as morning and evening prayer,
grace before and after meals,
the Liturgy of the Hours.

Sundays, centered on the Eucharist,
are kept holy primarily by prayer.
The cycle of the liturgical year
and its great feasts are also
basic rhythms
of the Christian's life of prayer.

Catechism of the Catholic Church ¶ 2698

TABLE OF CONTENTS

Prayers for Daily Use

The Sacraments

Devotions

Compline (Night Prayer)

Hymns

Prayer

is nothing else than being on
terms of friendship
with God.

St. Teresa of Avila

FOREWARD

The man who prays is fully alive. Whether it is in solitude or in community, the very essence of prayer draws one into the mystery of the Divine. When St. Paul urges us to "pray without ceasing" in his first letter to the Thessalonians, he presents a lofty goal that is also the deepest desire of every human heart – to converse and be in intimate union with God Himself.

While prayer that flows gracefully from the heart is a great gift, most people willingly admit their dependency on the spiritual giants of ages past. With its long and rich history, the Church has preserved a treasury of prayers that has passed through the generations. The prayers, liturgies, devotions, and hymns in the pages that follow are straight from the heart of this treasury – gathered in one place to help one develop a rhythm of unceasing prayer.

In an address to young people in 1979, Saint John Paul II spoke of prayer as the very strength of the Christian. He said that by lifting our minds and hearts to great ideals, "prayer gives light by which to see and to judge from God's perspective and from eternity." Without it, the Christian cannot see clearly, much less nourish the Life that is within.

Entering into the sanctuary of one's heart is an act of great faith, for faith is belief in that which we cannot see. With regular disciplines (like the daily "Angelus" depicted on the front cover of this book), prayer can become the very nourishment that draws the human soul into the depths of Trinitarian Love. By placing every moment of the day in the Sacred Heart of Jesus, life becomes a sacrifice of praise and prayer becomes the very rhythm of our heartbeat.

JIMMY MITCHELL
Solemnity of the Epiphany of the Lord
A.D. 2011

INTRODUCTORY REMARKS

The Church, in her heart, knows *why* we must pray: God is worthy of our prayer. The Church is the Bride of Christ, and her heart yearns for the Bridegroom, Jesus Christ, with such great love and devotion that her words cannot help but escape her lips without ceasing.

The Church, through her prudence, knows *when* to pray: in the cycles of human life; in celebration of the lives of the saints; in remembering the great works of God as He brought about salvation through His Son, our Lord Jesus Christ.

The Church, in her millennia of experience, knows *what* to pray: she has collected the best prayers of her saints from throughout the ages and recommended them to the Christian faithful as sure paths to perfect adoration, confession, thanksgiving, and supplication.

This book has been assembled to help you pray without ceasing – using the rhythms of prayer that the Bride of Christ, His Church, has always proposed to those who wish to know God, love God, and serve God with their whole heart, soul, mind, and strength. Within, you will find:

Prayers for Daily Use. Besides the Liturgy of the Hours, of which only a sample is included here, there have always been short prayers used by the faithful at certain times of the day: prayers said first thing in the morning; prayers said at sunset; prayers said before bed. There are some prayers that are so basic, that every Christian should know them by heart. Here, we recall the petition that Jesus gave us in the Lord's Prayer, "give us this day our daily bread," and we hunger for a deeper knowledge of our Lord and God.

PRAYERS FOR THE SACRAMENTS & ADORATION. Here the Church's perfect prayers, the Sacraments given by our Lord Himself, offer us a model of how to approach God. We can prepare for Mass and give thanks afterward; examine our conscience and make a good Confession; encounter the Body and Blood of Jesus in the Eucharist and sing His praises; sing the hymns and songs of the Church's sacred liturgy; and confess, through the Creeds, the one, true Faith.

DEVOTIONS. There are some prayers which have developed for so long, that they have acquired a special way of saying them: the Rosary, the Marian Antiphons, the Litanies, the Chaplet of Divine Mercy, the Stations of the Cross, and others. Each one of these prayers unlocks a beautiful aspect of God's mercy and love to his faithful. These prayers teach us what it means to be a devoted follower of Jesus Christ.

NIGHT PRAYER. In addition to the rhythms

introduced to the faithful by the Sacraments themselves, the Church sanctifies the whole of every day through prayers associated with the rising and setting of the sun. Here, we feature the last prayer of each day: the Office of Compline, or Night Prayer. This short, simple liturgical prayer is the voice of the Bride of Christ calling out to her Bridegroom for safety, rest, and protection as she descends beneath the gloomy shadows of sleep (recalling death), in joyful expectation of rising at the dawn of the new day (anticipating the resurrection to glory).

Hymnody. The book ends with adoration and praise of God through a collection of sacred hymns drawn from the Tradition of the Church. Many of them are translated into English from ancient languages, particularly Latin, the universal language of the Church.

As this rhythm develops, our very lives become a prayer as we sanctify the most ordinary moments – from time spent on work and with family to rest and recreation.

I will always remember hearing St. Paul's call to unceasing prayer for the first time. I will remember that I didn't know why to pray, when to pray, or what to pray. And, thanks be to God, I will always remember the night God brought me home to His Holy Church, giving me a treasury and rhythm of prayer that, by God's grace, I will keep for all eternity.

DILLON E. BARKER
Solemnity of the Immaculate Conception
of the Blessed Virgin Mary
A.D. 2010

gemitus·mei·adhesit
similis·factus
sum·pelicano
os·meum·carni·mee
I·N·R·I
Super dolorem
vulnerum·meorum

SETTING THE RHYTHM

If you're going to pray without ceasing, you're going to have to pray at specific times. It seems like an obvious statement – but it's one of those things that needs to be said. To begin following a regular rhythm of prayer, set aside specific times to spend a few moments with God every day. These don't have to be particularly long periods, but they do need to be serious moments where the only thing you're doing is offering God adoration, confession, thanksgiving, or supplication.

If you are a beginner, it's important that you take a realistic approach to acquiring a rhythm of prayer. If learning to sing or play an instrument, you wouldn't pick up a Stradivarius violin and expect to play the first chair's part in Beethoven's Ninth Symphony in one week; neither should you expect – or attempt, if you are a beginner – to take on everything suggested here in one fell swoop. Instead, try beginning with two or three of the disciplines, be faithful to them for a few weeks, and then try adding more.

As you grow in fidelity, set aside time every day for mental prayer, engaging in a silent dialogue with God. Start with 5-10 minutes a day. Find somewhere quiet and silently ask the Lord to speak to your heart, using Sacred Scripture and other aids to enlighten your prayer. Consider the words of the Prophet Samuel, "Speak, Lord, for your servant is listening."

And as you begin each day, recall the great tradition that associates each day with some aspect of our Faith: Sundays celebrate the Holy Trinity and the Resurrection. Mondays remind us to pray for the holy souls in Purgatory. Tuesdays help us to give thanks and ask for the intercession of our Guardian Angels. Wednesdays are the opportunity to recall St. Joseph, and ask for his prayers for a holy death.

Thursdays recall the Holy Eucharist and give us the chance to visit the Blessed Sacrament. Fridays remind us of the Passion and Death of our Lord, a great opportunity to pray the Stations of the Cross. Saturdays recall the Blessed Virgin Mary, a particularly apt time to pray the Rosary or some other Marian devotion.

The love of God is so profound that it demands a response. Let us pray for love of Him, for He is our only hope. *Oratio!*

Suggested Rhythm Check	
Daily	Morning Offering Mass (if possible) Mental Prayer Rosary (start with a decade) Angelus Spiritual Reading Examination of Conscience
Weekly	Sunday Mass
Monthly	Confession & Spiritual Direction Day of Recollection/Prayer
Yearly	Retreat

PRAYERS FOR DAILY USE

The religious sense
of the Christian people
has always found expression
in various forms of piety
surrounding the Church's sacramental life,
such as the veneration of relics,
visits to sanctuaries, pilgrimages, processions,
the stations of the cross, religious dances,
the rosary, medals[1], et cetera.

Catechism of the Catholic Church ¶ 1674

[1] *Cf. Council of Nicaea II: DS 601; 603; Council of Trent: DS 1822.*

R. DE CRAMER

BASIC PRAYERS

Sign of the Cross

In the Name of the Father,	*In nomine Patris*
and of the Son,	*et Filii,*
and of the Holy Spirit. Amen.	*et Spiritus Sancti. Amen.*

Our Father

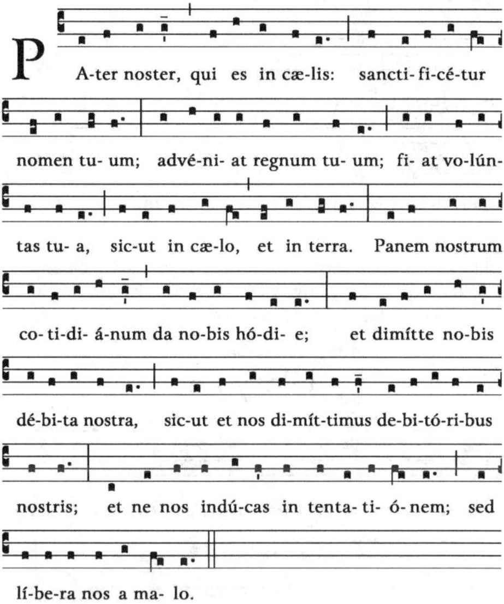

Our Father, who art in heaven, hallowed be thy name; thy kingdom come, thy will be done on earth as it is in heaven. Give us this day our daily bread; and forgive us our trespasses, as we forgive those who trespass against us; and lead us not into temptation, but deliver us from evil. Amen.

Hail Mary

Hail Mary, full of grace, the Lord is with thee. Blessed art thou amongst women and blessed is the fruit of thy womb Jesus. Holy Mary, Mother of God, pray for us sinners, now, and at the hour of our death. Amen.

Glory Be

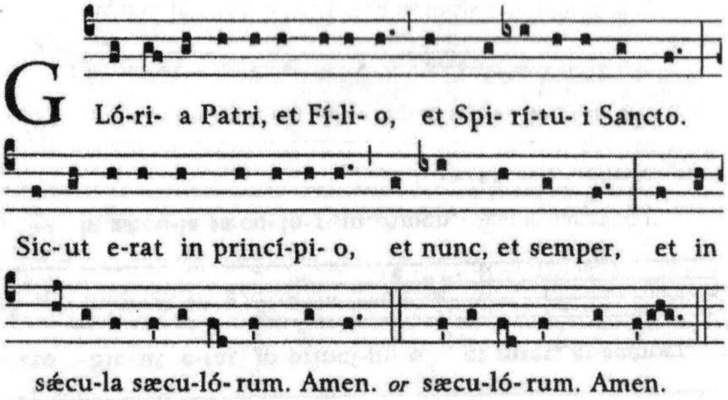

Glory be to the Father,
and to the Son,
and to the Holy Spirit.
As it was in the beginning,
is now, and ever shall be:
world without end.
Amen.

Gloria Patri,
et Filio,
et Spiritui Sancto.
Sicut erat in principio,
et nunc, et semper,
et in saecula saeculorum.
Amen.

Confiteor

I confess to almighty God and to you, my brothers and sisters, that I have greatly sinned, in my thoughts and in my words, in what I have done and in what I have failed to do, through my fault, through my fault, through my most grievous fault; therefore I ask blessed Mary ever-Virgin, all the Angels and Saints, and you, my brothers and sisters, to pray for me to the Lord our God.

Confiteor Deo omnipotenti, et vobis fratres, quia peccavi nimis cogitatione, verbo, opera et omissione, mea culpa, mea culpa, mea maxima culpa. Ideo precor beatam Mariam semper Virginem, omnes angelos et sanctos, et vos, fratres, orare pro me ad Dominum Deum nostrum.

St. Michael the Archangel

St. Michael the Archangel, defend us in battle; be our protection against the wickedness and snares of the devil. May God rebuke him, we humbly pray. And do thou, O prince of the heavenly host, by the power of God, cast into hell Satan and all the evil spirits, who prowl about the world seeking the ruin of souls. Amen.

Sancte Michael Archangele, defende nos in proelio, contra nequitiam et insidias diaboli esto praesidium. Imperet illi Deus, supplices deprecamur: tuque, Princeps militiae caelestis, Satanam aliosque spiritus malignos, qui ad perditionem animarum pervagantur in mundo, divina virtute, in infernum detrude. Amen.

Angel of God

Angel of God,
my guardian dear,
to whom God's love
commits me here;
ever this day be at my side,
to light and guard
to rule and guide. Amen.

Angele Dei,
qui custos es mei,
me tibi commissum
pietate superna;
hodie
illumina, custodi,
rege, et guberna. Amen.

Act of Faith

O my God, I firmly believe that you are one God in three divine persons, Father, Son and Holy Spirit; I believe that your divine Son became man and died for our sins, and that He shall come to judge the living and the dead. I believe these and all the truths which the holy Catholic Church teaches, because you have revealed them, who can neither deceive nor be deceived. Amen.

Act of Hope

O my God, relying on your almighty power and infinite mercy and promises, I hope to obtain pardon for my sins, the help of your grace, and life everlasting, through the merits of Jesus Christ, my Lord and Redeemer. Amen.

Act of Charity

O my God, I love you above all things with my whole heart and soul because you are all good and worthy of my love. I love my neighbor as myself for the love of you. I forgive all who have injured me and ask pardon of all whom I have injured. Amen.

MORNING PRAYERS

Morning Offering

O Jesus, through the Immaculate Heart of Mary, I offer You my prayers, works, joys and sufferings of this day for all the intentions of Your Sacred Heart, in union with the Holy Sacrifice of the Mass throughout the world, in reparation for my sins, for the intentions of all my relatives and friends, and in particular for the intentions of the Holy Father. Amen.

Direct, We Beg You, O Lord

Direct, we beg you, O Lord, our prayers and our actions by your holy inspirations; and carry them on by your gracious assistance, so that every work of ours may always begin with you, and through you come to completion. Amen.

Lord, God Almighty

Lord God Almighty, you have brought us safely to the beginning of this day. Defend us today by your mighty power, that we may not fall into any sin, but that all our words may so proceed and all our thoughts and actions be so directed, as to be always just in your sight. Through Christ our Lord. Amen.

Direct and Sanctify This Day

O Lord God, King of heaven and earth, may it please you this day to direct and to sanctify, to rule and to govern our hearts and our bodies, our thoughts, our words and our works, according to your law and in the doing of your commandments, that we, being helped by you, may here and hereafter worthily be saved and delivered by you, O Savior of the world, who lives and reigns forever and ever. Amen.

O Almighty God, Yours Are

O Almighty God, yours are the good things and the beauty of creation. Grant us this day to begin it joyfully in your name and to complete it lovingly in service to you and our brothers and sisters. Through Christ our Lord. Amen.

Three Hail Mary Devotion

St. Leonard of Port Maurice wrote that the faithful should pray three Hail Mary's in honor of the most holy Trinity and in honor of Mary Immaculate for the grace to avoid all mortal sins, especially sins against the virtue of chastity, at waking and before bed. St. Alphonsus Liguori also recommended this practice.

Hail Mary, full of grace... (3x)

Let us pray. By thy holy and Immaculate Conception, O Mary, pray for me, that my body may be pure and my soul holy; preserve me this day from mortal sin. Through Christ our Lord. Amen.

MIDDAY PRAYERS

Angelus

The Angelus is traditionally said at 6:00 a.m., at Noon, and at 6:00 p.m. in honor of the Incarnation of our Lord Jesus Christ. It is especially appropriate at Noon. During Eastertide, the Regina Caeli Devotion is used instead.

V. The angel of the Lord declared unto Mary.
R. And she conceived of the Holy Spirit.

V. Hail Mary... R. Holy Mary...

V. Behold the handmaid of the Lord.
R. Be it done unto me according to Thy word.

V. Hail Mary... R. Holy Mary...

V. And the Word was made flesh. (genuflect)
R. And dwelt among us.

V. Hail Mary... R. Holy Mary...

V. Pray for us, O holy Mother of God.
R. That we may be made worthy of the promises of Christ.

Let us pray: Pour forth, we beseech thee, O Lord, thy grace into our hearts; that we, to whom the incarnation of Christ, thy Son, was made known by the message of an angel, may by His passion and Cross be brought to the glory of his Resurrection. Through the same Christ, our Lord. Amen.

Angelus

An-ge- lus Dómi- ni nunti- á-vit Ma-rí- æ,
et concé- pit de Spí- ri- tu Sáncto.
Ave Marí-a, grá-ti- a pléna, Dóminus técum, benedícta
tu in muli-éribus, et benedíctus frúctus véntris tú-i, Jésus.
Sáncta Marí- a, máter Dé-i, óra pro nóbis pecca-tóribus,
nunc et in hóra mórtis nóstræ. Amen.
Ant. Ecce ancílla Dómi-ni, fí- at mí- hi
secúndum vérbum tú- um. A-ve Marí- a...

Ant. Et Vérbum cá- ro fáctum est,

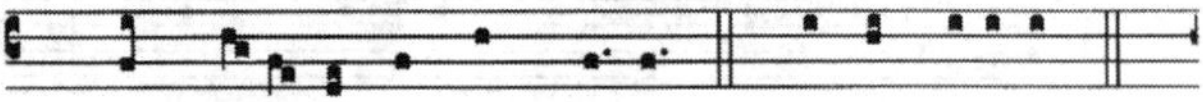

et habi- tá- vit in nó-bis. A-ve Marí- a...

℣. Ora pro nóbis, sáncta Dé- i Génitrix.

℟. Ut dígni effici- ámur promissi-ónibus Chrí-sti.

Orémus

GRÁTIAM tuam, quaésumus, Dómine, méntibus nostris infúnde: † ut qui, Ángelo nuntiánte, Christi Fílii tui incarnatiónem cognóvimus, * per passiónem ejus et crucem, ad resurrectiónis glóriam perducámur. Per eúmdem Christum Dóminum nostrum. ℟. **Amen.**

Regina Caeli

Said in place of the Angelus Devotion during Eastertide.

V. Queen of Heaven rejoice, alleluia:
R. For He whom you merited to bear, alleluia,

V. Has risen as He said, alleluia.
R. Pray for us to God, alleluia.

V. Rejoice and be glad, O Virgin Mary, alleluia.
R. Because the Lord is truly risen, alleluia.

Let us pray.

O God, who by the Resurrection of Thy Son, our Lord Jesus Christ, granted joy to the whole world: grant we beg Thee, that through the intercession of the Virgin Mary, His Mother, we may lay hold of the joys of eternal life. Through the same Christ our Lord. Amen.

Prayer for Midmorning

To you, O Lord, we humbly offer our prayers, that as you gave your Holy Spirit to the apostles, who were praying in the third hour, you would let us, by your loving kindness, share in this same grace. Through Christ our Lord. Amen.

Prayer for Midday

Almighty and eternal God, with whom nothing is darkness, nothing shadow: shine forth in us the splendor of your light, that we may understand your laws and commandments, and walk in your way with faithful and open hearts. Through Christ our Lord. Amen.

Prayer for Midafternoon

Grant to us who pray, we beg you, O Lord, that we may follow the example of the patience of your only-begotten Son, showing forth constant endurance in adversity. Through the same Christ our Lord. Amen.

EVENING PRAYERS

Brief Examination of Conscience at Bedtime

• MAKE THE SIGN OF THE CROSS and place yourself in the presence of God.

• ASK FOR LIGHT from our Lady, St. Joseph, and your guardian angel to acknowledge sins and virtues from throughout your day.

• CONSIDER THE THEOLOGICAL VIRTUES, honestly assessing where you did not exhibit these in your day:

FAITH. Did I make an honest effort to grow in the virtue of faith today? Did I say my usual prayers? Did I doubt God by relying on my own strength to deal with trials? Did I expose myself to anything that opposes or belittles the Catholic Faith? What did I do today to externally profess my faith?

HOPE. Did I make an honest effort to grow in the virtue of hope today? Did I dwell on my worries or offer them to God? Did I fail in the virtue of hope by my attachment to the things of this world? Did I see God's providence in everything that happened today? Am I justly confident that, with God's grace, I will enjoy eternal life? How often did I complain today, failing to hope in God's sovereignty?

CHARITY. Have I told each person of the holy Trinity that I love Him today? Did I embrace the cross each time

I had the chance to do so today? Have I failed to love my neighbor? Did I strive to love even those who seem difficult to love? Did I pray for anyone besides myself today? Did I lust after someone today? Did I covet today? Did I steal anything today? Did I do everything today for the love of God?

• MAKE AN ACT OF CONTRITION, sorrowfully asking for our Lord's pardon, and make a specific resolution for tomorrow, asking God's grace to keep it. Conclude with the Sign of the Cross.

Act of Contrition

O my God, I am heartily sorry for having offended you and I detest all my sins because of your just punishments, but most of all because they offend you, my God, who are all good and deserving of all my love. I firmly resolve, with the help of your grace, to sin no more and avoid the near occasions of sin. Amen.

Deus meus, ex toto corde paenitet me omnium meorum peccatorum, eaque detestor, quia peccando, non solum poenas a Te iuste statutas promeritus sum, sed praesertim quia offendi Te, summum bonum, ac dignum qui super omnia diligaris. Ideo firmiter propono, adiuvante gratia Tua, de cetero me non peccaturum peccandique occasiones proximas fugiturum. Amen.

Another Act of Contrition

My God, I am sorry for my sins with all my heart. In choosing to do wrong and failing to do good, I have sinned against you whom I should love above all things. I firmly intend, with your help, to do penance, to sin no more, and to avoid whatever leads me to sin. Our Savior Jesus Christ suffered and died for us. In his name, my God, have mercy. Amen.

Visit, We Beg You, O Lord

Visit, we beg you, O Lord, this dwelling, and drive from it all the snares of the enemy; let your holy Angels dwell here with us to keep us in peace; and let your blessing be always upon us. Through Christ our Lord. Amen.

Nighttime Offering by St. Alphonsus Liguori

Lord Jesus Christ, my God, I adore you and thank you for all the graces you have given me this day. I offer you my sleep and all the moments of this night, and I beseech you to keep me without sin. Therefore, I put myself within your sacred Side and under the mantle of our Lady, my Mother. Let your Holy Angels stand guard about me and keep me in peace; and let your blessing be upon me this night and forever. Amen.

THE SACRAMENTS

In the liturgy
and the celebration of the sacraments,
prayer and teaching are conjoined
with the grace of Christ
to enlighten and nourish all Christian activity.

As does the whole of the Christian life,
the moral life finds its source and summit
in the Eucharistic sacrifice.

Catechism of the Catholic Church ¶ 2031

THE MASS

Prayer of St. Ambrose

I draw near to the table of your most delectable banquet, dear Lord Jesus Christ. A sinner, I trust not in my own merit; but, in fear and trembling, I rely on your mercy and goodness. I have a heart and body marked by many grave offenses, and a mind and tongue that I have not guarded well. For this reason, God of loving kindness and awesome majesty, I, a sinner caught by many snares, seek safe refuge in you. For you are the fountain of mercy.

I would fear to draw near to you as my judge, but I seek you out as my Savior. Lord, I show you my wounds, and I let you see my shame. Knowing my sins are many and great, I have reason to fear. But I trust in your mercies, for they are beyond all numbering.

Look upon me with mercy, for I trust in you, my Lord Jesus Christ, eternal king, God and man, you who were crucified for mankind. Have mercy on me, you who never cease to make the fountain of your mercy flow, for I am full of sorrows and sins.

I praise you, the saving Victim offered on the wood of the cross for me and for all mankind. I praise the noble Blood that flows from the wounds of my Lord Jesus Christ, the precious Blood that washes away the sins of all the world. Remember, Lord, your creature, whom you have redeemed with your own Blood. I am sorry that I have sinned, and I long to put right what I have done.

Most kind Father, take away all my offenses and sins, so that, purified in body and soul, I may be made worthy to taste the Holy of holies.

And grant that this holy meal of your Body and Blood, which I intend to take, although I am unworthy, may bring forgiveness of my sins and wash away my guilt. May it mean the end of my evil thoughts and the rebirth of my better longings. May it lead me securely to live in ways that please you, and may it be a strong protection for body and soul against the plots of my enemies. Amen.

Prayer to Blessed Virgin Mary

Mother of mercy and of love, most blessed Virgin Mary, I, a poor and unworthy sinner, fly to thee with all my heart and all my affection. I implore thy loving kindness, that even as thou didst stand beside thy dear Son as He hung upon the Cross, so wilt thou also stand by me, a poor sinner, and beside all thy faithful people receiving the most sacred Body of thy Son. Grant us, that by thy grace, we may receive it worthily and fruitfully in the sight of the most high and undivided Trinity. Amen.

Prayer to All Angels & Saints

Prayer for priests, but may be adapted for personal use

Angels, Archangels, Thrones, Dominations, Principalities, Powers, heavenly Virtues, Cherubim and Seraphim; all Saints of God, holy men and women, and for you especially my patrons: deign to intercede for me that I may be worthy to offer this Sacrifice to almighty God, to the praise and glory of His name, for my own welfare and also that of all His holy Church. Amen.

Placeat Tibi

Prayer for priests, but may be adapted for personal use

May the tribute of my humble ministry be pleasing to you, Holy Trinity. Grant that the sacrifice which I, unworthy as I am, have offered in the presence of your majesty may be acceptable to you. Through your mercy may it bring forgiveness to me and to all for whom I have offered it: through Christ our Lord. Amen.

Prayer of St. Padre Pio After Communion

Stay with me, Lord, for it is necessary to have you present so that I do not forget you. You know how easily I abandon you. Stay with me, Lord, because I am weak and I need your strength, that I may not fall so often. Stay with me, Lord, for you are my life, and without you, I am without fervor. Stay with me, Lord, for you are my light, and without you, I am in darkness.

Stay with me, Lord, to show me your will. Stay with me, Lord, so that I hear your voice and follow you. Stay with me, Lord, for I desire to love you very much, and always be in your company. Stay with me, Lord, if you wish me to be faithful to you. Stay with me, Lord, for as poor as my soul is, I wish it to be a place of consolation for you, a nest of Love.

Stay with me, Jesus, for it is getting late and the day is coming to a close, and life passes, death, judgement, eternity approaches. It is necessary to renew my strength, so that I will not stop along the way and for that, I need you. It is getting late and death approaches. I fear the darkness, the temptations, the dryness, the cross, the sorrows. O how I need you, my Jesus, in this night of exile! Stay with me tonight, Jesus, in life with all its dangers, I need you. Let me recognize you as your disciples did at the breaking of bread, so that the Eucharistic Communion be the light which disperses the darkness, the force which sustains me, the unique joy of my heart.

Stay with me, Lord, because at the hour of my death, I want to remain united to you, if not by Communion, at least by grace and love. Stay with me, Jesus, I do not ask for divine consolation, because I do not merit it, but, the gift of your Presence, oh yes, I ask this of you! Stay with me, Lord, for it is you alone I look for. Your Love, your Grace, your Will, your Heart, your Spirit, because I love you and ask no other reward but to love you more and more. With a firm love, I will love you with all my heart while on earth and continue to love you perfectly during all eternity. Amen.

Prayer of St. Thomas Aquinas

Lord, Father all-powerful, and ever-living God, I thank you, for even though I am a sinner, your unprofitable servant, not because of my worth, but in the kindness of your mercy, you have fed me with the precious Body and Blood of your Son, our Lord Jesus Christ.

I pray that this holy communion may not bring me condemnation and punishment but forgiveness and salvation. May it be a helmet of faith and a shield of good will. May it purify me from evil ways and put an end to my evil passions. May it bring me charity and patience, humility and obedience, and growth in power to do good. May it be my strong defense against all my enemies, visible and invisible, and the perfect calming of all my evil impulses, bodily and spiritual. May it unite me more closely to you, the one true God and lead me safely through death to everlasting happiness with you.

And I pray that you will lead me, a sinner, to the banquet where you with your Son and the Holy Spirit, are true and perfect light, total fulfillment, everlasting joy, gladness without end, and perfect happiness to your saints. Amen.

Anima Christi

Soul of Christ, sanctify me. Body of Christ, save me. Blood of Christ, inebriate me. Water from the side of Christ, wash me. Passion of Christ, strengthen me. O good Jesus, hear me. Within Thy wounds, hide me. Separated from Thee let me never be. From the malignant enemy, defend me. At the hour of death, call me. To come to Thee, bid me, that I may praise Thee in the company of Thy Saints, for all eternity. Amen.

Anima Christi, sanctifica me. Corpus Christi, salva me. Sanguis Christi, inebria me. Aqua lateris Christi, lava me. Passio Christi, conforta me. O bone Iesu, exaudi me. Intra tua vulnera absconde me. Ne permittas me separari a te. Ab hoste maligno defende me. In hora mortis meae voca me. Et iube me venire ad te, ut cum Sanctis tuis laudem te in saecula saeculorum. Amen.

CONFESSION

Examination of Conscience

Adapted from Appendix III, Rite of Penance

Considerations Before Examination

1. TRUE REPENTANCE. What is my attitude to the Sacrament of Penance? Do I sincerely want to be set free from sin, to turn again to God, to begin a new life, and to enter into a deeper friendship with God? Or do I look at it as a burden, to be undertaken as seldom as possible?

2. SIN AGAINST THE SACRAMENT. Did I forget to mention, or deliberately conceal, any grave (mortal) sins in past confessions?

3. FOLLOWING THROUGH WITH PENANCE. Did I perform the penance I was given in my last confession? Did I make reparation for any injury to others? Have I tried to put into practice my resolution to lead a better life in keeping with the Gospel?

The Lord says: "You shall love the Lord your God with your whole heart."

4. HEART SET ON GOD. Is my heart set on God, so that I really love him above all things and am faithful to his commandments, as a son loves his father? Or am I more concerned about the things of this world? Have I a right intention in what I do?

5. FAITH. God spoke to us in his Son. Is my faith in God

firm and secure? Am I wholehearted in accepting the Church's teaching? Have I been careful to grow in my understanding of the faith, to hear God's Word, to listen to instructions on the faith, to avoid dangers to faith? Have I been always strong and fearless in professing my faith in God and the Church? Have I been willing to be known as a Christian in private and public life?

6. PRAYER. Have I prayed morning and evening? When I pray, do I really raise my mind and heart to God or is it a matter of words only? Do I offer God my difficulties, my joys, and my sorrows? Do I turn to God in time of temptation?

7. REVERENCE FOR GOD. Have I love and reverence for God's name? Have I offended him in blasphemy, swearing falsely, or taking his name in vain? Have I shown disrespect for the Blessed Virgin Mary and the saints?

8. REMEMBERING THE SABBATH. Do I keep Sundays and Holy Days of Obligation holy by taking part in the Mass with attention and devotion?

9. KEEPING GOD FIRST. Are there false gods that I worship by giving them greater attention and deeper trust than I give to God: money, ideology, superstition, or occult practices (Ouija boards, mediums, psychics, astrology, etc.)?

The Lord says: "Love one another as I have loved you."

10. LOVE OF NEIGHBOR. Have I genuine love for my neighbors? Or do I use them for my own ends, or do to them what I would not want done to myself? Have I given grave scandal by my words or actions?

11. FAMILY LIFE. In my family life, have I contributed to the well-being and happiness of the rest of the family by patience and genuine love? Have I been obedient to parents, showing them proper respect and giving them help in their spiritual and material needs? Have I been careful to give a Christian upbringing to my children, and to help them by good example and by exercising authority as a parent? Have I been faithful to my spouse, both in my heart and in my relations with others?

12. DUTY TO THE POOR. Do I share my possessions with the less fortunate? Do I do my best to help the victims of oppression, misfortune, and poverty? Or do I look down on my neighbor, especially the poor, the sick, the elderly, strangers, and people of other races?

13. DUTY TO THE CHURCH. Does my life reflect the mission I received in confirmation? Do I share in the apostolic and charitable works of the Church and in the life of my parish? Have I helped to meet the needs of the Church and of the world and prayed for them: for unity in the Church, for the spread of the Gospel among the nations, for peace and justice, etc.?

14. DUTY TO THE COMMUNITY. Am I concerned for the good and prosperity of the human community in which I

live, or do I spend my life caring only for myself? Do I share to the best of my ability in the work of promoting justice, morality, harmony, and love in human relations? Have I done my duty as a citizen? Have I paid my taxes? Do I vote regularly?

15. DUTY TO JUSTICE. In my work or profession am I just, hard-working, honest, serving society out of love for others? Have I paid a fair wage to my employees? Have I been faithful to my promises and contracts?

16. DUTY TO LEGITIMATE AUTHORITY. Have I obeyed legitimate authority and given it due respect? If I am in a position of responsibility or authority, do I use this for my own advantage or for the good of others, in a spirit of service?

17. TRUTH. Have I been truthful and fair, or have I injured others by deceit, calumny, detraction, rash judgment, or violation of a secret?

18. LIFE. Have I done violence to others by damage to life or limb, reputation, honor, or material possessions? Have I involved them in loss? Have I been responsible for advising an abortion or procuring one? Have I kept up hatred for others? Am I estranged from others through quarrels, enmity, insults, anger? Have I been guilty of refusing to testify to the innocence of another because of selfishness?

19. THEFT. Have I stolen the property of others? Have I desired it unjustly and inordinately? Have I damaged it? Have I made restitution of other people's property and made good their loss?

20. FORGIVENESS. If I have been injured, have I been ready to make peace and to forgive, for the love of Christ, or do I harbor hatred and the desire for revenge?

The Lord says: "Be perfect as your Father is perfect."

21. PURPOSE IN MY LIFE. Where is my life really leading me? Is the hope of eternal life my inspiration? Have I tried to grow in the life of the Spirit through prayer, reading the word of God and meditating on it, receiving the sacraments, self-denial?

22. VICE. Have I been anxious to control my vices, my bad inclinations and passions, e.g., envy, love of food and drink? Have I been proud and boastful, thinking myself better in the sight of God and despising others as less important than myself? Have I imposed my own will on others, without respecting their freedom and rights?

23. STEWARDSHIP OF GOD'S GIFTS. What use have I made of time, of health and strength, of the gifts God has given me to be used like the talents in the Gospel? Do I use them to become better every day? Or have I been lazy and too much given to leisure?

24. SUFFERING. Have I been patient in accepting the sorrows and disappointments of life? How have I performed mortification so as to "fill up what is wanting to the sufferings of Christ" (Col. 1:24)? Have I kept the precept of fasting and abstinence?

25. CHASTITY. Have I kept my senses and my whole body pure and chaste as a temple of the Holy Spirit consecrated for resurrection and glory, and as a sign of

God's faithful love for men and women, a sign that is seen most perfectly in the sacrament of matrimony?

26. SEXUAL PURITY. Have I dishonored my body by fornication, impurity, unworthy conversation or thoughts, evil desires, or actions? By myself or with others? With a person of the same or opposite sex? Have I given in to sensuality?

27. PURITY OF MIND AND HEART. Have I indulged in reading, conversation, shows, and entertainments that offend against Christian and human decency? Have I encouraged others to sin by my own failure to maintain these standards? Have I been faithful to the moral law in my married life?

28. FAITHFULNESS TO CONSCIENCE. Have I gone against my conscience out of fear or hypocrisy?

29. COMMITMENT TO BAPTISMAL PROMISES. Have I always tried to act in the true freedom of the sons of God according to the law of the Spirit, or am I the slave of forces within me?

RITE OF PENANCE

Reception of the Penitent

In the Name of the Father, † and of the Son, and of the Holy Spirit. Amen.

May God, who has enlightened every heart, help you to know your sins and trust in his mercy.

R. Amen.

Confession of Sins & Penance

If necessary, the Priest helps the Penitent to make an integral confession and gives him suitable counsel. He urges him to be sorry for his faults, reminding him that through the Sacrament of Penance, the Christian dies and rises with Christ and is thus renewed in the Paschal Mystery. The Priest proposes an Act of Penance which the Penitent accepts to make satisfaction for sin and to amend his life.

Prayer of the Penitent & Absolution

My God, I am sorry for my sins with all my heart. In choosing to do wrong and failing to do good, I have sinned against you whom I should love above all things. I firmly intend, with your help, to do penance, to sin no more, and to avoid whatever leads me to sin. Our Savior Jesus Christ suffered and died for us. In his name, my God, have mercy. Amen.

Then the Priest extends his hands over the Penitent's head (or at least extends his right hand) and says:

God, the Father of mercies, through the death and resurrection of his Son has reconciled the world to himself and sent the Holy Spirit among us for the forgiveness of sins; through the ministry of the Church may God give you pardon and peace, and I ABSOLVE YOU FROM YOUR SINS IN THE NAME OF THE FATHER, AND OF THE SON, AND OF THE HOLY SPIRIT.

R. Amen.

Proclamation of Praise & Dismissal

V. Give thanks to the Lord, for he is good.
R. His mercy endures forever.
V. The Lord has freed you from your sins. Go in peace.

PRAYERS FOR EUCHARISTIC ADORATION

O Salutaris Hostia

O Salutaris Hostia
Quae caeli pandis ostium
Bella premunt hostilia
Da robur, fer auxilium

Uni trinoque Domino
Sit sempiterna gloria
Qui vitam sine termino
Nobis donet in patria
Amen.

O saving Victim opening wide
The gate of heaven to all below
Our foes press on from every side
Thine aid supply, Thy strength bestow

To Thy great name be endless praise
Immortal Godhead, One in Three
Oh, grant us endless length of days
In our true native land with Thee
Amen.

Tantum Ergo

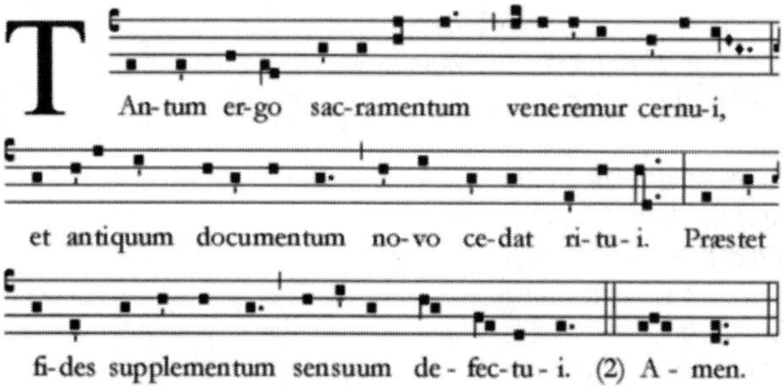

Genitori, Genitoque
Laus et iubilatio
Salus, honor, virtus quoque
Sit et benedictio
Procedenti ab utroque
Compar sit laudatio
Amen.

V. Panem de caelo praestitisti eis.
R. Omne delectamentum in se habentem.

Oremus. Deus, qui nobis sub sacramento mirabili, passionis tuae memoriam reliquisti: tribue, quaesummus, ita nos Corporis et Sanguinis tui sacra mysteria venerari, ut redemptionis tuae fructum in nobis iugiter sentiamus: Qui vivis and regnas in saecula saeculorum. Amen.

Down in adoration falling
Lo! the sacred Host we hail
Lo! o'er ancient forms departing
Newer rites of grace prevail
Faith for all defects supplying
Where the feeble senses fail

To the everlasting Father
And the Son Who reigns on high
With the Holy Spirit proceeding
Forth from each eternally
Be salvation, honor blessing
Might and endless majesty
Amen.

V. You have given them bread from heaven.
R. Having all sweetness within it

Let us pray. Lord Jesus Christ, you gave us the Eucharist as the Memorial of your suffering and death. May our worship of this sacrament of your Body and Blood help us to experience the salvation you won for us and the peace of the kingdom: where you live with the Father and the Holy Spirit: one God, forever and ever. Amen.

Divine Praises

Blessed be God.
Blessed be his Holy Name.
Blessed be Jesus Christ, true God and true man.
Blessed be the name of Jesus.
Blessed be his Most Sacred Heart.
Blessed be his Most Precious Blood.
Blessed be Jesus in the Most Holy Sacrament of the Altar.
Blessed be the Holy Spirit, the Paraclete.
Blessed be the great Mother of God, Mary most holy.
Blessed be her holy and Immaculate Conception.
Blessed be her glorious Assumption.
Blessed be the name of Mary, Virgin and Mother.
Blessed be Saint Joseph, her most chaste spouse.
Blessed be God in his angels and in his Saints.

May the heart of Jesus, in the Most Blessed Sacrament, be praised, adored, and loved with grateful affection, at every moment in all the tabernacles of the world, even unto the end of time. Amen.

Prayers for Visit to Blessed Sacrament

In the Name of the Father, † and of the Son, and of the Holy Spirit. Amen.

V. Let us adore forever:
R. The Most Holy Sacrament.

Repeat the above Antiphon 3 times.

Our Father… Hail Mary… Glory Be…

I adore you, O Jesus, true God and true Man, here present in the Holy Eucharist, humbly kneeling before you, united in spirit with all the faithful on earth and all the blessed in heaven. In deepest gratitude for so great a blessing, I love you, my Jesus, with my whole heart, for you are all perfect and worthy of love. Give me grace to nevermore in any way offend you, and grant that I, being refreshed by your Eucharistic presence here on earth, may be found worthy to come to the enjoyment, with Mary, of your eternal and ever blessed presence in heaven. Amen.

Then make an Act of Spiritual Communion.

Act of Spiritual Communion

O my Jesus, I believe that You are present in the Most Holy Sacrament. I love You above all things. I desire to receive You into my soul. Since I cannot receive You sacramentally at this moment, I ask you to come into my heart spiritually. I embrace You as if You were already there. I unite myself to You. Never permit me to be separated from You. Amen.

GOSPEL CANTICLES & LITURGICAL HYMNS

Benedictus

Luke 1:68-79 (Gospel Canticle at Morning Prayer)

Blessed † be the Lord, the God of Israel; he has come to his people and set them free. He has raised up for us a mighty savior, born of the house of his servant David. Through his holy prophets he promised of old that he would save us from our enemies, from the hands of all who hate us. He promised to show mercy to our fathers and to remember his holy covenant. This was the oath he swore to our father Abraham: to set us free from the hands of our enemies, free to worship him without fear, holy and righteous in his sight all the days of our life. You, my child, shall be called the prophet of the Most High; for you will go before the Lord to prepare his way, to give his people knowledge of salvation by the forgiveness of their sins. In the tender compassion of our God the dawn from on high shall break upon us, to shine on those who dwell in darkness and the shadow of death, and to guide our feet into the way of peace.

Magnificat

Luke 1:46b-55 (Gospel Canticle at Evening Prayer)

My † soul proclaims the greatness of the Lord, my spirit rejoices in God my Savior for he has looked with favor on his lowly servant. From this day all generations will call me blessed: the Almighty has done great things for me, and holy is his Name. He has mercy on those who fear him in every generation. He has shown the strength of his arm, he has scattered the proud in their conceit. He has cast down the mighty from their thrones, and has lifted up the lowly. He has filled the hungry with good things, and the rich he has sent away empty. He has come to the help of his servant Israel for he has remembered his promise of mercy, the promise he made to our fathers, to Abraham and his children forever.

Nunc Dimittis

Luke 2:29-32 (Gospel Canticle at Night Prayer)

Lord, † now you let your servant go in peace; your word has been fulfilled: my own eyes have seen the salvation which you have prepared in the sight of every people: a light to reveal you to the nations and the glory of your people Israel.

Te Deum

Liturgical Hymn at the Office of Readings (ca. 4th century A.D.)

You are God: we praise you; You are the Lord: we acclaim you; You are the eternal Father: All creation worships you. To you all angels, all the powers of heaven, Cherubim and Seraphim, sing in endless praise: Holy, holy, holy Lord, God of power and might, heaven and earth are full of your glory. The glorious company of apostles praise you. The noble fellowship of prophets praise you. The white-robed army of martyrs praise you. Throughout the world the holy Church acclaims you: Father, of majesty unbounded, your true and only Son, worthy of all worship, and the Holy Spirit, advocate and guide. You, Christ, are the king of glory, the eternal Son of the Father. When you became man to set us free you did not shun the Virgin's womb. You overcame the sting of death, and opened the kingdom of heaven to all believers. You are seated at God's right hand in glory. We believe that you will come, and be our judge. Come then, Lord, and help your people, bought with the price of your own blood, and bring us with your saints to glory everlasting.

V. Save your people, Lord, and bless your inheritance.
R. Govern and uphold them now and always.
V. Day by day we bless you.
R. We praise your name forever.
V. Keep us today, Lord, from all sin.
R. Have mercy on us, Lord, have mercy.
V. Lord, show us your love and mercy;
R. For we put our trust in you.
V. In you, Lord, is our hope:
R. And we shall never hope in vain.

Kyrie Eleison

Penitential Acclamation in the Introductory Rites of the Order of Mass

Lord, have mercy.	**Kyrie, eleison.**
Lord, have mercy.	Kyrie, eleison.
Christ, have mercy.	**Christe, eleison.**
Christ, have mercy.	Christe, eleison.
Lord, have mercy.	**Kyrie, eleison.**
Lord, have mercy.	Kyrie, eleison.

Gloria in Excelsis

Liturgical Hymn in the Introductory Rites of the Order of Mass

Glory to God in the highest, and on earth peace to people of good will. We praise you, we bless you, we adore you, we glorify you, we give you thanks for your great glory, Lord God, heavenly King, O God, almighty Father. Lord Jesus Christ, Only Begotten Son, Lord God, Lamb of God, Son of the Father, you take away the sins of the world, have mercy on us; you take away the sins of the world, receive our prayer; you are seated at the right hand of the Father, have mercy on us. For you alone are the Holy One, you alone are the Lord, you alone are the Most High, Jesus Christ, with the Holy Spirit, in the glory of God the Father. Amen.

G Ló-ri- a in excél-sis De- o. Et in terra pax homí-ni-bus bonæ
vo-luntá- tis. Laudá-mus te. Be-ne-dí-cimus te. Ado-rá-mus te.
Glo-ri- fi-cámus te. Grá-ti- as á-gimus ti- bi propter magnam gló-ri- am tu- am.
Dómi-ne De- us, Rex cæ-lé-stis, De- us Pa-ter omní-pot- ens. Dómi-ne Fi- li
u-ni-gé-ni-te Ie-su Chri-ste. Dómi-ne De- us, Agnus De- i, Fí- li- us
Pa- tris. Qui tol-lis peccá-ta mun-di, mi-se-ré- re no-bis. Qui tol-lis peccá-ta
múndi, súsci-pe depre-ca-ti- ó-nem no-stram. Qui se-des ad déxte-ram
Pá-tris, mi-se-ré-re nó-bis. Quó-ni- am tu so-lus sanctus. Tu so-lus Dómi-nus.
Tu so-lus Al-tís-simus, Iesu Chri-ste. Cum Sancto Spí-ri-tu,
in gló-ri- a De- i Pa- tris. A- men.

Sanctus

Post-Preface Acclamation in the Eucharistic Prayer of the Order of Mass

Holy, Holy, Holy Lord God of hosts.
Heaven and earth are full of your glory.
Hosanna in the highest.
Blessed is he who comes in the name of the Lord.
Hosanna in the highest.

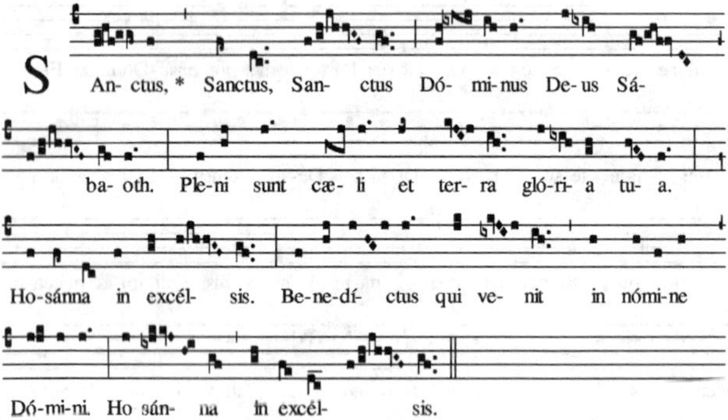

Mortem Tuam

Post-Consecration Acclamation in the Eucharistic Prayer of the Mass

We proclaim your Death, O Lord, and profess your Resurrection, until you come again.

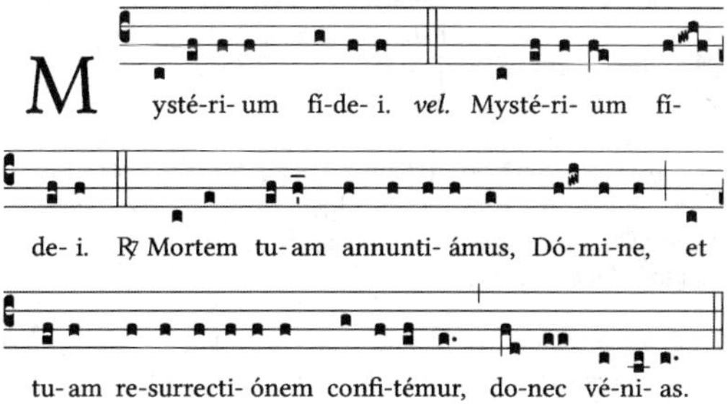

Agnus Dei

Antiphon at the Fraction of the Host in the Communion Rite of the Order of Mass

Lamb of God, you take away the sin of the world, have mercy on us.
Lamb of God, you take away the sin of the world, have mercy on us.
Lamb of God, you take away the sin of the world, grant us peace.

CREEDS OF THE CHURCH

Through the centuries many professions or symbols of faith have been articulated in response to the needs of the different eras: the creeds of the different apostolic and ancient Churches[1]*, e.g., the* Quicumque, *also called the Athanasian Creed*[2]*; the professions of faith of certain Councils, such as Toledo, Lateran, Lyons, Trent*[3]*; or the symbols of certain popes, e.g., the* Fides Damasi[4] *or the* Credo of the People of God *of Paul VI.*[5] *(Catechism of the Catholic Church ¶ 192)*

None of the creeds from the different stages in the Church's life can be considered superseded or irrelevant. They help us today to attain and deepen the faith of all times by means of the different summaries made of it. (Catechism of the Catholic Church ¶ 193)

Among all the creeds, two occupy a special place in the Church's life (Catechism of the Catholic Church ¶ 193) : the Apostles' Creed and the Niceno-Constantinopolitan Creed, which is usually called the Nicene Creed.

Apostles' Creed

The Apostles' Creed *is so called because it is rightly considered to be a faithful summary of the apostles' faith. It is the ancient baptismal symbol of the Church of Rome. Its great authority arises from this fact: it is "the Creed of the Roman Church, the See of Peter the first of the apostles, to which he brought the common faith."*[6] *(Catechism of the Catholic Church ¶ 194)*

The Apostles' Creed...constitutes, as it were, "the oldest Roman catechism." (Catechism of the Catholic Church 196)

1 Cf. DS 1-64.
2 Cf. DS 75-76.
3 Cf. DS 525-541; 800-802; 851-861; 1862-1870.
4 Cf. DS 71-72.
5 Paul VI, CPG (1968).
6 St. Ambrose, Expl. symb. 7: PL 17,1196.

I believe in God, the Father almighty, Creator of heaven and earth, and in Jesus Christ, his only Son, our Lord, who was conceived by the Holy Spirit, born of the Virgin Mary, suffered under Pontius Pilate, was crucified, died and was buried; he descended into hell; on the third day he rose again from the dead; he ascended into heaven, and is seated at the right hand of God the Father almighty; from there he will come to judge the living and the dead. I believe in the Holy Spirit, the holy catholic Church, the communion of saints, the forgiveness of sins, the resurrection of the body, and life everlasting. Amen.

Credo in Deum Patrem omnipotentem, Creatorem caeli et terrae. Et in Iesum Christum, Filium eius unicum, Dominum nostrum, qui conceptus est de Spiritu Sancto, natus ex Maria Virgine, passus sub Pontio Pilato, crucifixus, mortuus, et sepultus, descendit ad inferos, tertia die resurrexit a mortuis, ascendit ad caelos, sedet ad dexteram Dei Patris omnipotentis, inde venturus est iudicare vivos et mortuos. Credo in Spiritum Sanctum, sanctam Ecclesiam catholicam, sanctorum communionem, remissionem peccatorum, carnis resurrectionem, vitam aeternam. Amen.

Nicene Creed

The Niceno-Constantinopolitan *or* Nicene Creed *draws its great authority from the fact that it stems from the first two ecumenical Councils (in 325 and 381). It remains common to all the great Churches of both East and West to this day. (Catechism of the Catholic Church ¶ 195)*

I believe in one God, the Father almighty, maker of heaven and earth, of all things visible and invisible. I believe in one Lord Jesus Christ, the Only Begotten Son of God, born of the Father before all ages. God from God, Light from Light, true God from true God, begotten, not made, consubstantial with the Father; through him all things were made. For us men and for our salvation he came down from heaven, and by the Holy Spirit was incarnate of the Virgin Mary, and became man. For our sake he was crucified under Pontius Pilate, he suffered death and was buried, and rose again on the third day in accordance with the Scriptures. He ascended into heaven and is seated at the right hand of the Father. He will come again in glory to judge the living and the dead and his kingdom will have no end. I believe in the Holy Spirit, the Lord, the giver of life, who proceeds from the Father and the Son, who with the Father and the Son is adored and glorified, who has spoken through the prophets. I believe in one, holy, catholic and apostolic Church. I confess one Baptism for the forgiveness of sins and I look forward to the resurrection of the dead and the life of the world to come. Amen.

Credo in unum Deum, Patrem omnipotentem, factorem caeli et terrae, visibilium omnium et invisibilium. Et in unum Dominum Iesum Christum, Filium Dei unigenitum, et ex Patre natum ante omnia saecula. Deum de Deo, Lumen de Lumine, Deum verum de Deo vero, genitum non factum, consubstantialem Patri; per quem omnia facta sunt. Qui propter nos homines et propter nostram salutem descendit de caelis. Et incarnatus est de Spiritu Sancto ex Maria Virgine, et homo factus est. Crucifixus etiam pro nobis sub Pontio Pilato, passus et sepultus est, et resurrexit tertia die, secundum Scripturas, et ascendit in caelum, sedet ad dexteram Patris. Et iterum venturus est cum gloria, iudicare vivos et mortuos, cuius regni non erit finis. Et in Spiritum Sanctum, Dominum et vivificantem, qui ex Patre Filioque procedit. Qui cum Patre et Filio simul adoratur et conglorificatur: qui locutus est per prophetas. Et unam, sanctam, catholicam et apostolicam Ecclesiam. Confiteor unum baptisma in remissionem peccatorum. Et expecto resurrectionem mortuorum, et vitam venturi saeculi. Amen.

Athanasian Creed

The Athanasian Creed is one of the approved statements of the truths of the Faith, dating back to the fourth or fifth century. Modern scholarship indicates that it was not written by St. Athanasius, but its expressions and ideas reflect his influence. Some scholars think it may have been written or revised by St. Ambrose.

One of the symbols of the Faith approved by the Church and given a place in her liturgy [particularly on Trinity Sunday, in the Extraordinary Form of the Roman Rite], is a short, clear exposition of the doctrines of the Trinity and the Incarnation, with a passing reference to several other dogmas. Unlike most of the other creeds, or symbols, it deals almost exclusively with these two fundamental truths, which it states and restates in terse and varied forms so as to bring out unmistakably the trinity of the Persons of God, and the twofold nature in the one Divine Person of Jesus Christ. (James Sullivan, The Catholic Encyclopedia, 1907)

Whoever wishes to be saved must, above all, keep the Catholic faith. For unless a person keeps this faith whole and entire, he will undoubtedly be lost forever. This is what the Catholic faith teaches: we worship one God in the Trinity and the Trinity in unity. Neither confounding the Persons, nor dividing the substance. For there is one Person of the Father, another of the Son, another of the Holy Spirit. But the Father and the Son and the Holy Spirit have one divinity, equal glory, and coeternal majesty. What the Father is, the Son is, and the Holy Spirit is.

The Father is uncreated, the Son is uncreated, and the Holy Spirit is uncreated. The Father is boundless, the Son is boundless, and the Holy Spirit is boundless. The Father is eternal, the Son is eternal, and the Holy Spirit is eternal. Nevertheless, there are not three eternal beings, but one eternal being. So there are not three uncreated beings, nor three boundless beings, but one uncreated being and one boundless being.

Likewise, the Father is omnipotent, the Son is omnipotent, the Holy Spirit is omnipotent. Yet there are not three omnipotent beings, but one omnipotent being. Thus the Father is God, the Son is God, and the Holy Spirit is God. However, there are not three gods, but one God. The Father is Lord, the Son is Lord, and the Holy Spirit is Lord. However, there are not three lords, but one Lord. For as we are obliged by Christian truth to acknowledge every Person singly to be God and Lord, so too are we forbidden by the Catholic religion to say that there are three gods or lords.

The Father was not made, nor created, nor generated by anyone. The Son is not made, nor created, but begotten by the Father alone. The Holy Spirit is not made, nor created, nor generated, but proceeds from the Father and the Son. There is, then, one Father, not three Fathers; one Son, not three sons; one Holy Spirit, not three holy spirits. In this Trinity, there is nothing before or after, nothing greater or less. The entire three Persons are coeternal and coequal with one another. So that in all things, as has been said above, the Unity is to be worshiped in Trinity and the Trinity in Unity.

He, therefore, who wishes to be saved, must believe thus about the Trinity. It is also necessary for eternal salvation that he believes steadfastly in the incarnation of our Lord Jesus Christ. Thus the right faith is that we believe and confess that our Lord Jesus Christ, the Son of God, is both God and man. As God, He was begotten of the substance of the Father before time; as man, He was born in time of the substance of His Mother. He is perfect God; and He is perfect man, with a rational soul and human flesh. He is equal to the Father in His divinity, but inferior to the Father in His humanity. Although He is God and man, He is not two, but one Christ. And He is one, not because His divinity was changed into flesh, but because His humanity was assumed unto God. He is one, not by a mingling of substances, but by unity of person. As a rational soul and flesh are one man: so God and man are one Christ. He died for our salvation, descended into

Hell, and rose from the dead on the third day. He ascended into Heaven, sits at the right hand of God the Father almighty. From there He shall come to judge the living and the dead. At His coming, all men are to arise with their own bodies; and they are to give an account of their own deeds. Those who have done good deeds will go into eternal life; those who have done evil will go into the everlasting fire.

This is the Catholic faith. Everyone must believe it, firmly and steadfastly; otherwise he cannot be saved. Amen.

DEVOTIONS

Popular piety is a living reality
in and of the Church.
Its source is the constant presence
of the Spirit of God in the ecclesial community.
The mystery of Christ our Savior
is its reference point; the glory of God
and the salvation of man, its object;
its historical moment,
"the joyous encounter of the work
of evangelization and culture."
The Church sees popular piety
as "a true treasure of the People of God."

Directory on Popular Piety & the Liturgy no. 61

A Ω

STATIONS OF THE CROSS

Through them, the faithful movingly follow the final earthly journey of Christ: from the Mount of Olives, where the Lord, "in a small estate called Gethsemane" (Mk 14, 32), was taken by anguish (cf. Lk 22, 44) to Calvary where he was crucified between two thieves (cf. Lk 23, 33), to the garden where he was placed in a freshly hewn tomb (John 19, 40-42). It is a synthesis of various devotions that have arisen since the high middle ages: the pilgrimage to the Holy Land during which the faithful devoutly visit the places associated with the Lord's Passion; devotion to the three falls of Christ under the weight of the Cross; devotion to "the dolorous journey of Christ" which consisted in processing from one church to another in memory of Christ's Passion; devotion to the stations of Christ, those places where Christ stopped on his journey to Calvary because obliged to do so by his executioners or exhausted by fatigue, or because moved by compassion to dialogue with those who were present at his Passion. (Directory on Popular Piety & Liturgy, 131-32)

INTRODUCTION

In the Name of the Father, † and of the Son, and of the Holy Spirit. Amen.

Our help is in the Name of the Lord.
- Who made heaven and earth.

Glory be to the Father...

Lord, have mercy. - Lord, have mercy.

Christ, have mercy. - Christ, have mercy.

Lord, have mercy. - Lord, have mercy.

Our Father...

Let us pray.

God of power and mercy, in love you sent your Son that we might be cleansed of sin and live with you forever. Bless us as we gather to reflect on his suffering and death, that we may learn from his example the way we should go. Through Christ our Lord. Amen.

BEFORE EACH STATION

We adore you, O Christ, and we bless you.
- Because by your Holy Cross you have redeemed the world.

STATIONS

I. Jesus is condemned to death.
II. Jesus carries His cross.
III. Jesus falls the first time.
IV. Jesus meets His mother.
V. Simon of Cyrene helps Jesus carry the cross.
VI. Veronica wipes the face of Jesus.
VII. Jesus falls the second time.
VIII. Jesus meets the women of Jerusalem.
IX. Jesus falls the third time.
X. Jesus clothes' are taken away.
XI. Jesus is nailed to the cross.
XII. Jesus dies on the cross.
XIII. Jesus is taken down from the cross.
XIV. Jesus is laid in the tomb.

AFTER EACH STATION

Our Father... Hail Mary... Glory Be...

CONCLUSION

Lord, have mercy.	- Lord, have mercy.
Christ, have mercy.	- Christ, have mercy.
Lord, have mercy.	- Lord, have mercy.

Let us pray. Lord Jesus Christ, your passion and death is the sacrifice that unites earth and heaven and reconciles all people to you. May we who have faithfully reflected on these mysteries follow in your steps and so come to share your glory in heaven where you live and reign with the Father and the Holy Spirit, one God, forever and ever. Amen.

STABAT MATER

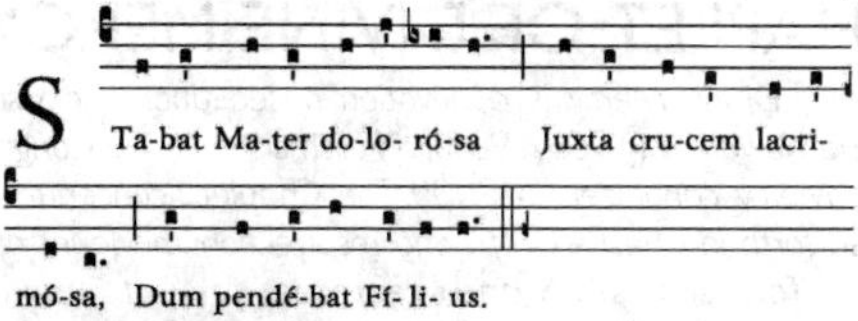

2. Cujus ánimam geméntem,
Contristátam et doléntem
Pertransívit gládius.

3. O quam tristis et afflícta
Fuit illa benedícta
Mater Unigéniti!

4. Quæ mærébat et dolébat,
Pia Mater, dum vidébat
Nati pœnas ínclyti.

5. Quis est homo qui non fleret,
Matrem Christi si vidéret
In tanto supplício?

6. Quis non posset contristári,
Christi matrem contemplári
Doléntem cum Fílio?

7. Pro peccátis suæ gentis,
Vidit Jesum in torméntis,
Et flagéllis súbditum.

8. Vidit suum dulcem natum
Moriéndo desolátum,
Dum emísit spíritum.

9. Eia Mater, fons amóris,
Me sentíre vim dolóris
Fac, ut tecum lúgeam.

10. Fac ut árdeat cor meum
In amándo Christum Deum,
Ut sibi compláceam.

1. At the cross her station keeping, stood the mournful Mother weeping, close to Jesus to the last. 2. Through her heart, His sorrow sharing, all His bitter anguish bearing, now at length the sword had passed. 3. Oh, how sad and sore distress'd, was that Mother highly blest, of the sole-begotten One! 4. Christ above in torment hangs; she beneath beholds the pangs, of her dying glorious Son. 5. Is there one who would not weep, whelm'd in miseries so deep Christ's dear Mother to behold? 6. Can the human heart refrain, from partaking in her pain, in that Mother's pain untold? 7. Bruised, derided, cursed, defiled, she beheld her tender Child, all with bloody scourges rent. 8. For the sins of His own nation, saw Him hang in desolation, till His spirit forth He sent. 9. O thou Mother! fount of love! Touch my spirit from above, make my heart with thine accord. 10. Make me feel as thou hast felt; make my soul to glow and melt, with the love of Christ my Lord.

CHAPLET OF DIVINE MERCY

The Chaplet of Divine Mercy is a devotion based upon the visions of St. Mary Faustina Kowalska (1905-1938), a Polish sister of the Congregation of Our Lady of Mercy canonized in 2000. The Chaplet "concentrates on the mercy poured forth in Christ's death and resurrection: the fount of the Holy Spirit, who forgives sins and restores joy at having been redeemed" (Directory on Popular Piety & the Liturgy, 154). It is prayed using normal Rosary beads.

INTRODUCTION: In the Name of the Father, † and of the Son, and of the Holy Spirit. Amen.

OPTIONAL OPENING PRAYER: You expired, Jesus, but the source of life gushed forth for souls, and the ocean of mercy opened up for the whole world. O Fount of Life, unfathomable Divine Mercy, envelop the whole world and empty yourself out upon us. O Blood and Water, which gushed forth from the Heart of Jesus as a fountain of Mercy for us, I trust in you! Amen.

Our Father... Hail Mary... Apostles' Creed...

ON THE "OUR FATHER" BEADS

V. Eternal Father, I offer you the Body and Blood, Soul and Divinity of your dearly beloved Son, our Lord Jesus Christ,

R. In atonement for our sins and those of the whole world.

ON THE "HAIL MARY" BEADS

V. For the sake of his sorrowful Passion:

R. Have mercy on us and the whole world.

AT THE END

The following is said three times:

V. Holy God, Holy Mighty One, Holy Immortal One:

R. Have mercy on us and the whole world.

OPTIONAL CLOSING PRAYER: Eternal God, in whom mercy is endless and the treasury of compassion inexhaustible, look kindly upon us and increase your mercy in us, that in difficult moments we might not despair nor become despondent, but with great confidence submit ourselves to your holy will, which is Love and Mercy itself. Amen.

AVE VERUM CORPUS

Hail, true Body
Born of the Virgin Mary,
Who truly suffered, sacrificed
On the Cross for man,
Whose pierced side overflowed
With water and blood,
Be for us a foretaste
In the test of death.

LITANY OF HUMILITY

This Litany was composed by Cardinal Merry del Val. He would often recite it after celebrating the Holy Sacrifice of the Mass.

O Jesus, meek and humble of heart, **hear me.**
From the desire of being esteemed… **deliver me Jesus.**
From the desire of being loved,
From the desire of being extolled,
From the desire of being honored,
From the desire of being praised,
From the desire of being preferred to others,
From the desire of being consulted,
From the desire of being approved,
From the fear of being humiliated,
From the fear of being despised,
From the fear of suffering rebukes,
From the fear of being calumniated,
From the fear of being forgotten,
From the fear of being ridiculed,
From the fear of being wronged,
From the fear of being suspected…

That others may be loved more than I…
Jesus grant me the grace to desire it.
That others may be esteemed more than I,
That in the opinion of the world others may increase and I may decrease,
That others may be chosen and I set aside,
That others may be praised and I unnoticed,
That others may be preferred to me in everything,
That others become holier than I provided that I may become as holy as I should…

PRAYERS TO MARY

The Rosary: Structure & Prayers

The Rosary of the Virgin Mary, which gradually took form in the second millennium under the guidance of the Spirit of God, is a prayer loved by countless Saints and encouraged by the Magisterium. Simple yet profound, it still remains a prayer of great significance, destined to bring forth a harvest of holiness. It blends easily into the spiritual journey of the Christian life, which, after two thousand years, has lost none of the freshness of its beginnings and feels drawn by the Spirit of God to "set out into the deep" (duc in altum!) in order once more to proclaim, and even cry out, before the world that Jesus Christ is Lord and Savior, "the way, and the truth and the life" (Jn 14:6), "the goal of human history and the point on which the desires of history and civilization turn" (Gaudium et Spes, 45).

The Rosary, though clearly Marian in character, is at heart a Christocentric prayer. In the sobriety of its elements, it has all the depth of the Gospel message in its entirety, of which it can be said to be a compendium (Marialis Cultus, 2). It is an echo of the prayer of Mary, her perennial "Magnificat" for the work of the redemptive Incarnation which began in her virginal womb. With the Rosary, the Christian people sit at the school of Mary and are led to contemplate the beauty of the face of Christ and to experience the depths of his love. Through the Rosary the faithful receive abundant grace, as though from the very hands of the Mother of the Redeemer. (John Paul II, *Rosarium Virginis Mariae*)

INTRODUCTION

In the Name of the Father, † and of the Son, and of the Holy Spirit. Amen.

AT THE CRUCIFIX

Apostles' Creed (p. 58)

ON THE LARGE BEADS

Our Father (p. 15)

ON THE SMALL BEADS

Hail Mary (p. 16)

BEFORE EACH DECADE

Announce the Mystery upon which you will be meditating (see below). Pope John Paul II also recommended reading a brief passage of Scripture related to the Mystery before proceeding to the prayers.

AFTER EACH DECADE

Glory Be (p. 16)

FATIMA PRAYER

O my Jesus, forgive us our sins and save us from the fires of Hell. Lead all souls to heaven, especially those in most need of thy mercy.

AT THE END

Hail holy Queen, Mother of mercy, our life, our sweetness, and our hope. To thee do we cry, poor banished children of Eve. To thee do we send up our sighs, mourning and weeping in this valley of tears.
Turn then, most gracious Advocate, thine eyes of mercy toward us. And after this our exile show unto us the blessed fruit of thy womb, Jesus.
O clement, O loving, O sweet Virgin Mary.

V. Pray for us, O Holy Mother of God.
R. That we may be made worthy of the promises of Christ.

Let us pray.

O God, who by the life, death, and resurrection of your only-begotten Son, has purchased for us the rewards of eternal salvation: grant, we beseech you, that meditating on these mysteries of the most holy Rosary of the Blessed Virgin Mary, we may imitate what they contain and obtain what they promise, through the same Christ our Lord. Amen.

The Mysteries of the Rosary

Announcing each Mystery [of the Rosary], is, as it were, to open up a scenario on which to focus our attention. The words direct the imagination and the mind towards a particular episode or moment in the life of Christ. In order to supply a Biblical foundation and greater depth to our meditation, it is helpful to follow the announcement of the mystery with the proclamation of a related Biblical passage, long or short, depending on the circumstances. No other words can ever match the efficacy of the inspired Word. As we listen, we are certain that this is the Word of God, spoken for today and spoken "for me." (John Paul II, *Rosarium Virginis Mariae*)

The Joyful Mysteries

Mondays and Saturdays

1. The Incarnation of our Lord Jesus Christ
   (Mt. 1:18, Lk. 1:26-38)
2. The Visitation of our Lady to St. Elizabeth
   (Lk. 1:39-45)
3. The Nativity of our Lord Jesus Christ
   (Lk. 2:1-20)
4. The Presentation of Jesus in the Temple
   (Lk. 2:22-38)
5. The Finding of the Child Jesus Teaching in the Temple
   (Lk. 2:41-52)

The Luminous Mysteries

Thursdays

1. The Baptism of Jesus in the River Jordan
   (Mt. 3:13-17, Mk. 1:4-11)
2. The Miracle at the Wedding in Cana of Galilee
   (Jn. 2:1-11)
3. The Proclamation of the Kingdom
   (Mt. 4:12-25, Lk. 7:47-48)
4. The Transfiguration of Jesus
   (Mt. 17:1-9, Lk. 9:28-36)
5. The Institution of the Eucharist
   (Lk. 22:14-20, Jn. 13:1)

The Sorrowful Mysteries

Tuesdays and Fridays

1. The Agony in the Garden
   (Mt. 26:36-56)
2. The Scourging at the Pillar
   (Mk. 15:1-15)
3. The Crowning with Thorns
   (Mk. 15:16-20, Mt. 27:27-31)
4. The Carrying the Cross to Golgotha
   (Lk. 23:26-32, Mk. 10:17-21)
5. The Crucifixion
   (Jn. 19:17-30, Mt. 27:35-56)

The Glorious Mysteries
Wednesdays and Sundays

1. The Resurrection of our Lord
   (Mt. 28:1-15, Mk. 16:1-18)
2. The Ascension of our Lord
   (Acts 1:3-11)
3. The Descent of the Holy Spirit
   (Acts 2:1-21)
4. The Assumption of our Lady
   (Song 2:10-13, Lk. 1:46-50)
5. The Coronation of our Lady
   (Rev. 12:1, Ps. 44:14-16, Jud. 15:10)

Litany of Loreto

Litanies are to be found among the prayers to the Blessed Virgin recommended by the Church. These consist in a long series of invocations of Our Lady, which follow in a uniform rhythm, thereby creating a stream of prayer characterized by insistent praise and supplication. The invocations, generally very short, have two parts: the first of praise (Virgo clemens), the other of supplication (Ora pro nobis). The Litanies are important acts of homage to the Blessed Virgin Mary. The Litany of Loreto [has been] repeatedly recommended by the Roman Pontiffs. Pope Leo XIII prescribed that the Litany of Loreto should follow the recitation of the Rosary during the month of October. (Directory on Popular Piety & the Liturgy, 203)

Lord, have mercy. *Lord, have mercy.*
Christ, have mercy. *Christ, have mercy.*
Lord, have mercy. *Lord, have mercy.*
Christ, hear us. *Christ graciously hear us.*
God, the Father of heaven, *have mercy on us.*

God the Son, Redeemer of the world, *have mercy on us.*
God the Holy Ghost, *have mercy on us.*
Holy Trinity, one God, *have mercy on us.*

Holy Mary, *pray for us…*
Holy Mother of God,
Holy Virgin of virgins,
Mother of Christ,
Mother of the Church,
Mother of divine grace,
Mother most pure,
Mother most chaste,
Mother inviolate,
Mother undefiled,
Mother most amiable,
Mother most admirable,
Mother of good counsel,
Mother of our Creator,
Mother of our Savior,
Virgin most prudent,
Virgin most venerable,
Virgin most renowned,
Virgin most powerful,
Virgin most merciful,
Virgin most faithful,
Mirror of justice,
Seat of wisdom,
Cause of our joy,
Spiritual vessel,
Vessel of honor,
Singular vessel of devotion,

Mystical rose,
Tower of David,
Tower of ivory,
House of gold,
Ark of the covenant,
Gate of heaven,
Morning star,
Health of the sick,
Refuge of sinners,
Comforter of the afflicted,
Help of Christians,
Queen of Angels,
Queen of Patriarchs,
Queen of Prophets,
Queen of Apostles,
Queen of Martyrs,
Queen of Confessors,
Queen of Virgins,
Queen of all Saints,
Queen conceived without original sin,
Queen assumed into heaven,
Queen of the most holy Rosary,
Queen of the family,
Queen of Peace, *pray for us.*

Lamb of God, who takes away the sins of the world,
spare us, O Lord.
Lamb of God, who takes away the sins of the world,
graciously hear us, O Lord.
Lamb of God, who takes away the sins of the world,
have mercy on us.

V. Pray for us, O Holy Mother of God.
R. That we may be made worthy of the promises of Christ.

Let us pray. Grant, we beseech you, O Lord God, unto us your servants, that we may rejoice in continual health of mind and body; and, by the glorious intercession of Blessed Mary ever Virgin, may be delivered from present sadness, and enter into the joy of your eternal gladness. Through Christ our Lord. Amen.

Consecration to Mary

by St. Padre Pio (1887-1968)

O Mary, Virgin most powerful and Mother of mercy, Queen of Heaven and Refuge of sinners, we consecrate ourselves to your Immaculate Heart. We consecrate to you our very being and our whole life; all that we have, all that we love, all that we are. To you we give our bodies, our hearts and our souls; to you we give our homes, our families, our country. We desire that all that is in us and around us may belong to you, and may share in the benefits of your motherly benediction.

And that this act of consecration may be truly efficacious and lasting, we renew this day at your feet the promises of our Baptism and our first Holy Communion. We pledge ourselves to profess courageously and at all times the truths, of our Holy Faith, and to live as Catholics who are duly submissive to all the directions of the Pope and the Bishops in communion with him. We pledge ourselves to keep the commandments of God and his Church, in particular to keep holy the Lord's day. We likewise pledge ourselves to make the consoling practices of the Christian religion, and above all, Holy Communion, an integral part of our lives, in so far as we shall be able to do so.

Finally, we promise you, O glorious Mother of God and loving Mother of all, to devote ourselves whole-heartedly to your service, in order to hasten and assure, through the sovereignty of your Immaculate Heart, the coming of the kingdom of the Sacred Heart of your adorable Son, in our own hearts and in the hearts of all, in our country and in all the world, as in heaven, so on earth. Amen.

Memorare

Remember, O most gracious Virgin Mary, that never was it known that anyone who fled to thy protection, implored thy help, or sought thy intercession was left unaided. Inspired with this confidence, I fly unto thee, O Virgin of virgins, my Mother. To thee do I come, before thee I stand, sinful and sorrowful. O Mother of the Word Incarnate, despise not my petitions, but in thy mercy, hear and answer me. Amen.

Alma Redemptoris Mater

Said from Evening Prayer I of the First Sunday of Advent through the Feast of the Presentation.

O loving Mother of our Redeemer, gate of heaven, star of the sea, hasten to aid thy fallen people who strive to rise once more. thou who brought forth thy holy Creator, all creation wond'ring, yet remainest ever Virgin, taking from Gabriel's lips that joyful "Hail!": be merciful to us sinners.

Ave Regina Caelorum

Said after the Feast of the Presentation through Good Friday.

Welcome, O Lady of Angels Hail! thou root, hail! thou gate from whom unto the world, a light has arisen: Rejoice, O glorious Virgin, lovely beyond all others. Farewell, most beautiful maiden, and pray for us to Christ.

Regina Caeli

Said during Eastertide.

℣. Gáude et laetáre, Vírgo María, allelúia.
℟. Quia surréxit Dóminus vére, allelúia.

V. Queen of Heaven, rejoice, alleluia.
R. For He whom you did merit to bear, alleluia.
V. Has risen, as he said, alleluia.
R. Pray for us to God, alleluia.
V. Rejoice and be glad, O Virgin Mary, alleluia.
R. For the Lord has truly risen, alleluia.

Let us pray. O God, who gave joy to the world through the resurrection of thy Son, our Lord Jesus Christ; grant, we beseech thee, that through his Mother, the Virgin Mary, we may obtain the joys of everlasting life. Through the same Christ our Lord. Amen.

Salve Regina

Said from Evening Prayer I of Trinity Sunday through Advent.

SAINT PRAYERS

St. Joseph

From the 1st century A.D.

O, St. Joseph, whose protection is so great, so strong, so prompt before the throne of God, I place in you all my interests and desires. O, St. Joseph, do assist me by your powerful intercession, and obtain for me from your divine Son all spiritual blessings, through Jesus Christ, our Lord. So that, having engaged here below your heavenly power, I may offer my thanksgiving and homage to the most loving of Fathers.

O, St. Joseph, I never weary of contemplating you, and Jesus asleep in your arms; I dare not approach while he reposes near your heart. Press him in my name and kiss his fine head for me and ask him to return the kiss when I draw my dying breath. St. Joseph, patron of departing souls, pray for me. Amen.

St. Gertrude the Great

Eternal Father, I offer thee the Most Precious Blood of thy Divine Son, Jesus, in union with the Masses said throughout the world today, for all the holy souls in Purgatory, for sinners everywhere, for sinners in the universal church, those in my own home and within my family. Amen.

St. Augustine of Hippo

Prayer to the Holy Spirit from the 5th century

Breathe in me, O Holy Spirit
that my thoughts may all be holy.
Act in me, O Holy Spirit
that my work, too, may be holy.
Draw my heart, O Holy Spirit
that I love but what is holy.
Strengthen me, O Holy Spirit
to defend all that is holy.
Guard me, then, O Holy Spirit
that I always may be holy.
Amen.

St. Francis of Assisi

Lord, make me an instrument of your peace.
Where there is hatred, let me sow love.
Where there is injury, pardon.
Where there is doubt, faith.
Where there is despair, hope.
Where there is darkness, light.
Where there is sadness, joy.

O Divine Master, grant that I may not seek so much to be consoled, as to console; to be understood, as to understand; to be loved, as to love. For it is in giving that we receive. It is in pardoning that we are pardoned. And it is in dying that we are born to eternal life. Amen.

St. Ignatius of Loyola

From the 16th century

Lord Jesus Christ, take all my freedom, my memory, my understanding, and my will. All that I have and cherish you have given me. I surrender it all to be guided by your will. Your grace and your love are wealth enough for me. Give me these, Lord Jesus, and I ask for nothing more. Amen.

St. John Bosco

For the protection of young people

O glorious Saint John Bosco, who in order to lead young people to the feet of the divine Master and to mold them in the light of faith and Christian morality didst heroically sacrifice thyself to the very end of thy life and didst set up a proper religious institute destined to endure and to bring to the farthest boundaries of the earth thy glorious work, obtain also for us from Our Lord a holy love for young people who are exposed to so many seductions in order that we may generously spend ourselves in supporting them against the snares of the devil, in keeping them safe from the dangers of the world, and in guiding them, pure and holy, in the path that leads to God. Amen.

St. Thomas Aquinas

STUDENT PRAYER: Creator of all things, true source of light and wisdom, origin of all being, graciously let a ray of your light penetrate the darkness of my understanding. Take from me the double darkness in which I have been born, an obscurity of sin and ignorance. Give me a keen understanding, a retentive memory, and the ability to grasp things correctly and fundamentally. Grant me the talent of being exact in my explanations and the ability to express myself with thoroughness and charm. Point out the beginning, direct the progress, and help in the completion. I ask this through Christ our Lord. Amen.

THE PRAYER TO SAINT THOMAS FOR PURITY:
Chosen lily of innocence, pure St. Thomas, who kept chaste the robe of Baptism and became an angel in the flesh after being girded by two angels, I implore you to commend me to Jesus, the Spotless Lamb, and to Mary, the Queen of Virgins. Gentle protector of my purity, ask them that I, who wear the holy sign of your victory over the flesh, may also share your purity, and after imitating you on earth may at last come to be crowned with you among the angels. Amen.

THE PRAYER OF SAINT THOMAS FOR PURITY:
Dear Jesus, I know that every perfect gift, and especially that of chastity, depends on the power of your providence. Without you a mere creature can do nothing. Therefore, I beg you to defend by your grace the chastity and purity of my body and soul. And if I have ever sensed or imagined anything that could stain my chastity and purity, blot it out, Supreme Lord of my powers, that I may advance with a pure heart in your love and service, offering myself on the most pure altar of your divinity all the days of my life. Amen.

The purity prayers are prayed daily along with 15 Hail Mary's.

St. Josemaría Escrivá

For personal meditation

Before: My Lord and my God, I firmly believe that you are here, that you see me, that you hear me. I adore you with profound reverence; I ask your pardon for my sins and the grace to make this time of prayer fruitful. My Immaculate Mother, St. Joseph, my father and lord, my guardian angel: intercede for me.

After: I thank you, my God, for the good resolutions, affections, and inspirations that you have communicated to me in this time of prayer. I ask your help to put them into effect. My Immaculate Mother, St. Joseph, my father and lord, my guardian angel: intercede for me.

Litany of the Saints

The Litanies of the Saints contain elements deriving from both the liturgical tradition and from popular piety. They are expressions of the Church's confidence in the intercession of the Saints and an experience of the communion between the Church of the heavenly Jerusalem and the Church on her earthly pilgrim journey. (Directory on Popular Piety & the Liturgy)

Lord, have mercy. *Lord, have mercy.*
Christ, have mercy. *Christ, have mercy.*
Lord, have mercy. *Lord, have mercy.*
Christ, hear us. *Christ graciously hear us.*

God, the Father of heaven, *have mercy on us.*
God the Son, Redeemer of the world, *have mercy on us.*
God the Holy Ghost, *have mercy on us.*
Holy Trinity, one God, *have mercy on us.*

Holy Mary, *pray for us...*
Holy Mother of God,
Holy Virgin of virgins,
St. Michael,
St. Gabriel,
St. Raphael,
All you Holy Angels and Archangels,
St. John the Baptist,
St. Joseph,
All you Holy Patriarchs and Prophets,
St. Peter,
St. Paul,
St. Andrew,
St. James,
St. John,
St. Thomas,
St. James,
St. Philip,
St. Bartholomew,
St. Matthew,
St. Simon,
St. Jude,
St. Matthias,
St. Barnabas,
St. Luke,
St. Mark,
All you holy Apostles and Evangelists,
All you holy Disciples of the Lord,
All you holy Innocents,
St. Stephen,
St. Lawrence,

St. Vincent,
Sts. Fabian and Sebastian,
Sts. John and Paul,
Sts. Cosmos and Damian,
All you holy Martyrs,
St. Sylvester,
St. Gregory,
St. Ambrose,
St. Augustine,
St. Jerome,
St. Martin,
St. Nicholas,
All you holy Bishops and Confessors,
All you holy Doctors,
St. Anthony,
St. Benedict,
St. Bernard,
St. Dominic,
St. Francis,
All you holy Priests and Levites,
All you holy Monks and Hermits,
St. Mary Magdalene,
St. Agatha,
St. Lucy,
St. Agnes,
St. Cecilia,
St. Catherine,
St. Anastasia,
St. Clare,
All you holy Virgins and Widows,
All you holy Saints of God, *intercede for us.*

Lord, be merciful, *Lord, save your people...*
From all evil,
From all sin,
From your wrath,
From a sudden and unprovided death,
From the snares of the devil,
From anger, hatred, and all ill-will,
From the spirit of fornication,
From lightning and tempest,
From the scourge of earthquake,
From plague, famine, and war,
From everlasting death,
By the mystery of your holy Incarnation,
By your Coming,
By your Birth,
By your Baptism and holy fasting,
By your Cross and Passion,
By your Death and Burial,
By your holy Resurrection,
By your wonderful Ascension,
By the coming of the Holy Spirit,
On the day of judgment, *Lord, save your people.*

Be merciful to us sinners, *Lord, hear our prayer...*
That you will spare us,
That you will pardon us,
That it may please you to bring us to true penance,
Guide and protect your holy Church,
Preserve in holy religion the Pope, and all those in Holy Orders,

Humble the enemies of holy Church,
Give peace and unity to the whole Christian people,
Bring back to the unity of the Church all those who are straying, and bring all unbelievers to the light of the Gospel,
Strengthen and preserve us in your holy service,
Raise our minds to desire the things of Heaven,
Reward all our benefactors with eternal blessings,
Deliver our souls from eternal damnation, and the souls of our brethren, relatives, and benefactors,
Give and preserve the fruits of the earth,
Grant eternal rest to all the faithful departed,
That it may please you to hear and heed us, Jesus, Son of the Living God, *Lord, hear our prayer.*

Lamb of God, who takes away the sins of the world, *spare us, O Lord!*
Lamb of God, who takes away the sins of the world, *graciously hear us, O Lord!*
Lamb of God, who takes away the sins of the world, *have mercy on us.*

Christ, hear us, *Christ, graciously hear us.*
Lord Jesus, hear our prayer. *Lord Jesus, hear our prayer.*
Lord, have mercy. *Lord, have mercy.*
Christ, have mercy. *Christ, have mercy.*
Lord, have mercy. *Lord, have mercy.*

MENTAL PRAYER

A Short Method of Meditation (Abridged)
from St. Francis de Sales' *Introduction to the Devout Life*
written for St. Jane Frances de Chantal

1. The Presence of God

Make use of one or other of these methods for placing yourself in the Presence of God before you begin to pray; do not try to use them all at once, but take one at a time, and that briefly and simply.

First, a lively earnest realization that His Presence is universal; that is to say, that he is everywhere, and in all, and that there is no place, nothing in the world, devoid of his Most Holy Presence, so that, even as birds on the wing meet the air continually, we, let us go where we will, meet with that Presence always and everywhere. It is a truth which all are ready to grant, but all are not equally alive to its importance.

The second way of placing yourself in this Sacred Presence is to call to mind that God is not only present in the place where you are, but that he is very specially present in your heart and mind, which he kindles and inspires with his Holy Presence, abiding there as heart of your heart, spirit of your spirit. Just as the soul animates the whole body, and every member thereof, but abides especially in the heart, so God, while present everywhere, yet makes his special abode with our spirit.

The third way is to dwell upon the thought of our Lord, who in his Ascended Humanity looks down upon all men, but most particularly on all Christians, because they are his children; above all, on those who pray, over whose doings he keeps watch. Nor is this any mere imagination, it is very truth, and although we see him not, he is looking down upon us.

The fourth way is simply to exercise your ordinary imagination, picturing the Savior to yourself in his Sacred Humanity as if he were beside you just as we are wont to think of our friends, and fancy that we see or hear them at our side. But when the Blessed Sacrament of the Altar is there, then this Presence is no longer imaginary, but most real; and the sacred species are but as a veil from behind which the Present Savior beholds and considers us, although we cannot see him as he is.

2. Invocation

Your soul, having realized God's Presence, will prostrate itself with the utmost reverence, acknowledging its unworthiness to abide before his Sovereign Majesty; and yet knowing that he of his Goodness would have you come to him, you must ask of him grace to serve and worship him in this your meditation.

3. Imagination

Following upon these two ordinary points, there is a third, which is not necessary to all meditation, called by some the local representation, and by others the interior picture. It is simply kindling a vivid picture of the mystery to be meditated within your imagination, even as though you were actually beholding it. For instance, if you wish to meditate upon our Lord on his Cross, you will place yourself in imagination on Mount Calvary, as though you saw and heard all that occurred there during the Passion; or you can imagine to yourself all that the Evangelists describe as taking place where you are.

4. Considerations

After this exercise of the imagination, we come to that of the understanding: for meditations, properly so called, are certain considerations by which we raise the affections to God and heavenly things. Now meditation differs therein from study and ordinary methods of thought which have not the Love of God or growth in holiness for their object, but some other end, such as the acquisition of learning or power of argument. So, when you have, as I said, limited the efforts of your mind within due bounds, whether by the imagination, if the subject be material, or by propositions, if it be a spiritual subject, you will begin to form reflections or considerations after the pattern of the meditations I have already sketched for you. And if your mind finds sufficient matter, light and fruit wherein to rest in any one consideration, dwell upon it, even as the bee, which hovers over one flower so long as it affords honey. But if you do not find wherewith to feed your mind, after a certain reasonable effort, then go on to another consideration, only be quiet and simple, and do not be eager or hurried.

5. Affections and Resolutions

Meditation excites good desires in the will, or sensitive parts of the soul, such as love of God and of our neighbor, a craving for the glory of Paradise, zeal for the salvation of others, imitation of our Lord's Example, compassion, thanksgiving, fear of God's wrath and of judgment, hatred of sin, trust in God's Goodness and Mercy, shame for our past life; and in all such affections you should pour out your soul as much as possible. If you want help in this, turn to some simple book of devotions, the *Imitation of Christ*, the *Spiritual Combat*, or whatever you find most helpful to your individual wants.

But you must not stop short in general affections, without turning them into special resolutions for your own correction and amendment. For instance, meditating on Our Dear Lord's First Word from the Cross, you will no doubt be roused to the desire of imitating him in forgiving and loving your enemies. But that is not enough, unless you bring it to some practical resolution, such as, I will not be angered any more by the annoying things said of me by such or such a neighbor, nor by the slights offered me by such; but rather I will do such and such things in order to soften and conciliate them. In this way, you will soon correct your faults, whereas mere general resolutions would take but a slow and uncertain effect.

6. The Conclusion and Spiritual Bouquet

The meditation should be concluded by three acts, made with the utmost humility. First, an act of thanksgiving; thanking God for the affections and resolutions with which he has inspired you, and for the Mercy and Goodness He has made known to you in the mystery you have been meditating. Secondly, an act of oblation, by which you offer your affections and resolutions to God, in union with his Own Goodness and Mercy, and the Death and Merits of his Son. The third act is one of petition, in which you ask God to give you a share in the Merits of his Dear Son, and a blessing on your affections and resolutions, to the end that you may be able to put them in practice. You will further pray for the Church, and all her Ministers, your relations, friends, and all others, using the Our Father as the most comprehensive and necessary of prayers.

Besides all this, I bade you gather a little bouquet of devotion, and what I mean is this. When walking in a beautiful garden most people are wont to gather a few flowers as they go, which they keep, and enjoy their scent during the day. So, when the mind explores some mystery in meditation, it is well to pick out one or more points that have specially arrested the attention, and are most likely to be helpful to you through the day, and this should be done at once before quitting the subject of your meditation.

LECTIO DIVINA

From Brother Guigo II's *The Ladder of Four Rungs* (A.D. 1150)

When I was at hard at work one day, thinking on the spiritual work needed for God's servants, four such spiritual works came to my mind, these being: reading; meditation; prayer; contemplation. This is the ladder for those in cloisters, and for others in the world who are God's lovers, by means of which they can climb from earth to heaven. It is a marvelously tall ladder, but with just four rungs, the one end standing on the ground, the other thrilling into the clouds and showing the climber heavenly secrets.

Understand now what the four staves of this ladder are, each in turn. **Reading** is busily looking on Holy Scripture with all one's will and wit. **Meditation** is a studious searching with the mind to know what was before concealed. **Prayer** is a devout desiring of the heart to get what is good and avoid what is evil. **Contemplation** is the lifting up of the heart to God, tasting somewhat of the heavenly sweetness. Reading seeks, meditation finds, prayer asks, contemplation feels. That is to say, "Seek and you shall find: knock and the door will be opened for you." That means also, seek through reading, and you will find holy meditation in your thinking; and knock through praying, and the doors shall be opened to you to enter through heavenly contemplation to feel what you desire.

Reading puts as it were whole food into your mouth; meditation chews it and breaks it down; prayer finds its savor; contemplation is the sweetness that so delights and strengthens. Reading is like the bark, the shell; meditation like the nut; prayer is in the desiring; and contemplation is in the delight of the great sweetness.

Reading is the first ground that precedes and leads one into meditation; meditation seeks busily, and also with deep thought digs and delves deeply to find that treasure; and because it cannot be attained by itself alone, then he sends us into prayer that is mighty and strong. And so prayer rises to God, and there one finds the treasure one so fervently desires, that is the sweetness and delight of contemplation. And then contemplation comes and yields the harvest of the labor of the other three through a sweet heavenly dew, that the soul drinks in delight and joy.

From Pope Benedict XVI's Post-Synodal Exhortation, *Verbum Domini*
"The Basic Steps of Lectio Divina"

1. It opens with the **reading** (*lectio*) of a text, which leads to a desire to understand its true content: what does the biblical text say in itself? Without this, there is always a risk that the text will become a pretext for never moving beyond our own ideas.

2. Next comes **meditation** (*meditatio*), which asks: what does the biblical text say to us? Here, each person, individually but also as a member of the community, must let himself or herself be moved and challenged.

3. Following this comes **prayer** (*oratio*), which asks the question: what do we say to the Lord in response to his word? Prayer, as petition, intercession, thanksgiving and praise, is the primary way by which the word transforms us.

4. Finally, lectio divina concludes with **contemplation** (*contemplatio*), during which we take up, as a gift from God, his own way of seeing and judging reality, and ask ourselves what conversion of mind, heart and life is the Lord asking of us? In the Letter to the Romans, Saint Paul tells us: "Do not be conformed to this world, but be transformed by the renewal of your mind, that you may prove what is the will of God, what is good and acceptable and perfect" (12:2). Contemplation aims at creating within us a truly wise and discerning vision of

reality, as God sees it, and at forming within us "the mind of Christ" (1 Cor 2:16). The word of God appears here as a criterion for discernment: it is "living and active, sharper than any two-edged sword, piercing to the division of soul and spirit, of joints and marrow, and discerning the thoughts and intentions of the heart" (Heb 4:12).

We do well also to remember that the process of lectio divina is not concluded until it arrives at **action** (*actio*), which moves the believer to make his or her life a gift for others in charity.

We find the supreme synthesis and fulfillment of this process in the Mother of God. For every member of the faithful, Mary is the model of docile acceptance of God's word, for she "kept all these things, pondering them in her heart" (Lk 2:19; cf. 2:51); she discovered the profound bond which unites, in God's great plan, apparently disparate events, actions and things.

ASPIRATIONS

Sundry collections of ejaculatory prayer have been put forth, which are doubtless very useful, but I should advise you not to tie yourself to any formal words, but rather to speak with heart or mouth whatever springs forth from the love within you, which is sure to supply you with all abundance. There are certain utterances which have special force, such as the ejaculatory prayers of which the Psalms are so full, and the numerous loving invocations of Jesus which we find in the Song of Songs. Many hymns too may be used with the like intention, provided they are sung attentively. In short, just as those who are full of some earthly, natural love are ever turning in thought to the beloved one, their hearts overflowing with tenderness, and their lips ever ready to praise that beloved object; comforting themselves in absence by letters, carving the treasured name on every tree – so those who love God cannot cease thinking of him, living for him, longing after him, speaking of him, and fain would they grave the Holy Name of Jesus in the hearts of every living creature they behold. (St. Francis de Sales)

Some Examples

From Sacred Scripture & Tradition

- O God, have mercy on me, a sinner. (Luke 18:13)
- Blessed be the Name of the Lord!
- May the Most Blessed Sacrament be praised and adored forever.
- Veni Sancte Spiritus, veni per Mariam!
- Stay with us, O Lord. (Luke 24:29)
- We adore Thee, O Christ, and we bless Thee; because by Thy holy Cross Thou hast redeemed the world.
- O Lord, increase our faith. (Luke 17:5)
- Teach me to do Thy will, because Thou art my God. (Psalm 142:10)
- O Heart of Jesus, burning with love for us, inflame our hearts with love for Thee.

- My Lord and my God. (John 20:28)
- O Heart of Jesus, I place my trust in Thee.
- O Heart of Jesus, all for Thee.
- O Lord, save us, we are perishing. (Matthew 8:25)
- Thou art the Christ, the Son of the living God. (Matthew 16:16)
- Mother of Sorrows, pray for us.
- My Mother, my Hope.
- All for thee, Most Sacred Heart of Jesus!
- Send, O Lord, laborers into Thy harvest. (Matt 9:38)
- May the Virgin Mary together with her loving Child bless us.
- Hail, O Cross, our only hope.
- All you holy men and women of God, intercede for us.
- Pray for us, O Holy Mother of God, that we may be made worthy of the promises of Christ.
- Father, into Thy hands I commend my spirit. (Luke 23:46; Psalm 30:6)
- Merciful Lord Jesus, grant them everlasting rest.
- Jesus, meek and humble of heart, make my heart like unto thine!
- My Jesus, mercy!
- Thanks be to God! (Deo gratias!)
- O Mary, conceived without sin, pray for us who have recourse to thee!
- Sacred Heart of Jesus, I trust in Thee!
- Sacred Heart of Jesus, Thy kingdom come!
- Sweet Heart of Jesus, be my love!
- Holy Trinity, one God, have mercy on us!
- As the Lord wills!
- Thy will be done! (Fiat voluntas tua!)

BLESSINGS

Blessing Before a Meal

Bless us, † O Lord, and these Thy gifts which we are about to receive from Thy bounty; through Christ our Lord. Amen.

BEFORE MIDDAY MEAL:
May the King of everlasting glory make us partakers of the heavenly table. Amen.

BEFORE EVENING MEAL:
May the King of everlasting glory lead us to the banquet of life eternal. Amen.

Thanksgiving After a Meal

We give you thanks, almighty God, for all Thy benefits, who lives and reigns forever and ever. Amen.

V. May the Lord grant us his peace.
R. And life everlasting. Amen.

Blessing on a Birthday

INTRODUCTORY RITES

In the name of the Father, † and of the Son, and of the Holy Spirit. Amen.

Blessed be the name of the Lord.
- Now and forever.

READING FROM THE WORD OF GOD

A reading from the letter of Saint Paul to the Philippians (1:3-11); Alternate Readings: 1 Thessalonians 3:9-11. Matthew 5:1-12.

I give thanks to my God at every remembrance of you, praying always with joy in my every prayer for all of you, because of your partnership for the gospel from the first day until now. I am confident of this, that the one who began a good work in you will continue to complete it until the day of Christ Jesus. It is right that I should think this way about all of you, because I hold you in my heart, you who are all partners with me in grace, both in my imprisonment and in the defense and confirmation of the gospel. For God is my witness, how I long for all of you with the affection of Christ Jesus. And this is my prayer: that your love may increase ever more and more in knowledge and every kind of perception, to discern what is of value, so that you may be pure and blameless for the day of Christ, filled with the fruit of righteousness that comes through Jesus Christ for the glory and praise of God.

The word of the Lord.
- Thanks be to God.

PRAYER OF BLESSING FOR ADULTS

A minister who is a priest or deacon says the prayer of blessing with hands outstretched over the one who is to be blessed; a lay minister says the prayer with hands joined.

God of all creation,
we offer you grateful praise for the gift of life.
Hear the prayers of N., your servant,
who recalls today the day of his/her birth
and rejoices in your gifts of life and love,
family and friends.

Bless him/her with your presence
and surround him/her with your love
that he/she may enjoy many happy years,
all of them pleasing to you.

We ask this through Christ our Lord.
- Amen.

PRAYER OF BLESSING FOR CHILDREN

Loving God,
you created all the people of the world
and you know each of us by name.
We thank you for N., who today celebrates his/her birthday.
Bless him/her with your love and friendship
that he/she may grow in wisdom, knowledge, and grace.
May he/she love his/her family always and be faithful to his/her friends.

Grant this through Christ our Lord.
- Amen.

Blessing of the Sick

INTRODUCTORY RITES

In the name of the Father, † and of the Son, and of the Holy Spirit. Amen.

Our help is in the name of the Lord.
- Who made heaven and earth.

READING FROM THE WORD OF GOD

A reading from the second letter of Saint Paul to the Corinthians (1:3-4); Alternate Reading: Mt 11:28-30

Blessed be the God and Father of our Lord Jesus Christ, the Father of compassion and God of all encouragement, who encourages us in our every affliction, so that we may be able to encourage those who are in any affliction with the encouragement with which we ourselves are encouraged by God.

The word of the Lord.
- Thanks be to God.

PRAYER OF BLESSING

As circumstances suggest, a minister who is a priest or deacon may lay hands on the sick person while saying the prayer of blessing; a lay minister may trace the sign of the cross on the sick person's forehead while saying the prayer.

For one sick person:

Lord and Father, almighty and eternal God,
by your blessing you give us strength and support in our frailty:
turn with kindness toward your servant, N.

Free him/her from all illness and restore him/her to health,
so that in the sure knowledge of your goodness,
he/she will gratefully bless your holy Name.

We ask this through Christ our Lord.
- Amen.

Blessing of Travelers

INTRODUCTORY RITES

In the name of the Father, † and of the Son, and of the Holy Spirit. Amen.

Our help is in the name of the Lord.
- Who made heaven and earth.

READING FROM THE WORD OF GOD

A reading from the book of Tobit (4:19a); Alternate Reading: Jn 14:6

At all times bless the Lord God, and ask him to make all your paths straight and to grant success to all your endeavors and plans.

The word of the Lord.
- Thanks be to God.

PRAYER OF BLESSING

All-powerful and ever-living God,
when Abraham left his own land
and departed from his own people,
you kept him safe all through his journey.
Protect us, who are also your servants:
walk by our side to help us;
be our companion and strength on the road
and our refuge in every adversity.
Lead us, O Lord,
so that we will reach our destination in safety
and happily return to our homes.

We ask this through Christ our Lord.
- Amen.

or

May God bless you with every heavenly blessing
and give you a safe journey;
wherever life leads you,
may you may find him there to protect you.

We ask this through Christ our Lord.
- Amen.

INDULGENCES

Since the faithful departed now being purified are also members of the same communion of saints, one way we can help them is to obtain indulgences for them, so that the temporal punishments due for their sins may be remitted. (Catechism of the Catholic Church ¶ 1479)

An Introduction

Catechism of the Catholic Church ¶ *1471-3*

"An indulgence is a remission before God of the temporal punishment due to sins whose guilt has already been forgiven, which the faithful Christian who is duly disposed gains under certain prescribed conditions through the action of the Church which, as the minister of redemption, dispenses and applies with authority the treasury of the satisfactions of Christ and the saints."[1]

"An indulgence is partial or plenary according as it removes either part or all of the temporal punishment due to sin."[2] The faithful can gain indulgences for themselves or apply them to the dead.[3] (*Catechism of the Catholic Church* ¶ 1471)

To understand this doctrine and practice of the Church, it is necessary to understand that sin has a *double consequence*. Grave sin deprives us of communion with God and therefore makes us incapable of eternal life, the privation of which is called the "eternal punishment" of sin. On the other hand every sin, even venial, entails an unhealthy attachment to creatures, which must be purified either here on earth, or after death in the state called Purgatory. This purification frees one from what is called the "temporal punishment" of sin. These two punishments must not be conceived of as a kind of vengeance inflicted by God from without, but as following from the very nature of sin. A conversion which proceeds

1 Paul VI, apostolic constitution, Indulgentiarum doctrina, Norm 1.
2 Indulgentiarum doctrina, Norm 2; Cf. Norm 3.
3 CIC, can. 994. 84

from a fervent charity can attain the complete purification of the sinner in such a way that no punishment would remain.[1] (*Catechism of the Catholic Church* ¶ 1472)

The forgiveness of sin and restoration of communion with God entail the remission of the eternal punishment of sin, but temporal punishment of sin remains. While patiently bearing sufferings and trials of all kinds and, when the day comes, serenely facing death, the Christian must strive to accept this temporal punishment of sin as a grace. He should strive by works of mercy and charity, as well as by prayer and the various practices of penance, to put off completely the "old man" and to put on the "new man."[2] (*Catechism of the Catholic Church* ¶ 1473)

Requirements

From the Manual of Indulgences (1999 Latin); (2006 English)

[N17] ¶1. In order to be capable of gaining indulgences one must be baptized, not excommunicated, and in the state of grace at least at the completion of the prescribed works.

¶2. To gain an indulgence, one must have at least the general intention of doing so and must carry out the enjoined works at the stated time and in due fashion, according to the sense of the grant.

[N18.] ¶1. A plenary indulgence can be acquired once only in the course of a day; a partial indulgence can be acquired multiple times.

¶2. The faithful however can obtain the plenary indulgence *at the hour of death*, even if they have already gained one on the same day.

[N19.] The work prescribed for acquiring a plenary indulgence connected with a church or oratory consists of a devout visit during which an Our Father and the Creed are recited, unless other directives have been laid down.

1 Cf. Council of Trent (1551): DS 1712-1713; (1563): 1820.
2 Eph 4:22, 24.

[N20.] ¶1. To gain a plenary indulgence, in addition to excluding all attachment to sin, even venial sin, it is necessary to perform the indulgenced work and fulfill the following three conditions: sacramental confession, Eucharistic Communion, and prayer for the intention of the Sovereign Pontiff.

[N25.] Hierarchs or local ordinaries can grant permission to the faithful over whom they exercise legitimate authority and who live in places where it is impossible or at least very difficult to go to confession or Communion to gain a plenary indulgence without confession and Communion, provided they have contrition for their sins and have the intention of receiving these Sacraments as soon as possible.

Some Examples

See Manual of Indulgences for complete list

1. Praying the Rosary in a Church or as a family
2. Reading of Sacred Scripture for ½ hour
3. Praying Stations of the Cross in a Church
4. Adoration of Blessed Sacrament for ½ hour
5. Visiting a Parish Church on its feast day
6. Assisting in the adoration of the Cross on Good Friday
7. Devoutly receiving a Papal Blessing (even by radio or in a live broadcast)
8. Attending the closing Mass of a Eucharistic Congress
9. Pilgrimage to a Patriarchal Basilica in Rome and reciting one Our Father and the Creed (as part of a group making a pilgrimage to the basilica, or at least with the purpose of expressing during the visit filial submission to the Roman Pontiff)
10. At one's First Communion, or if you devoutly assist at someone else's First Communion
11. At the first Mass of newly ordained Priest
12. Attending a Parish Mission with devotion and attention to the sacred preaching
13. On special days (with prayers for certain feasts and solemnities)
14. The moment of death

NIGHT PRAYER

The mystery of Christ,
his Incarnation and Passover,
which we celebrate in the Eucharist
especially at the Sunday assembly,
permeates and transfigures
the time of each day, through the celebration
of the Liturgy of the Hours,
"the divine office."[1] (CCC 1174)
The faithful who celebrate
the Liturgy of the Hours
are united to Christ our high priest,
by the prayer of the Psalms,
meditation on the Word of God,
and canticles and blessings (CCC 1196).

[1] *Cf. SC, Ch. IV, 83-101.*

SUNDAY

God, † come to my assistance.
– Lord, make haste to help me.

Glory to the Father, and to the Son, and to the Holy Spirit:
– as it was in the beginning, is now, and will be forever. Amen.
(Alleluia)

EXAMINATION OF CONSCIENCE

CONFITEOR (p. 17)

HYMN

PSALMODY

Ant. Night holds no terrors for me sleeping under God's wings.

Psalm 91 - Safe in God's sheltering care
I have given you the power to tread upon serpents and scorpions (Luke 10:19).

He who dwells in the shelter of the Most High
and abides in the shade of the Almighty
says to the Lord: "My refuge,
my stronghold, my God in whom I trust!"

It is he who will free you from the snare
of the fowler who seeks to destroy you;
he will conceal you with his pinions
and under his wings you will find refuge.

You will not fear the terror of the night
nor the arrow that flies by day,
nor the plague that prowls in the darkness
nor the scourge that lays waste at noon.

A thousand may fall at your side,
ten thousand fall at your right,
you, it will never approach;
his faithfulness is buckler and shield.

Your eyes have only to look
to see how the wicked are repaid,
you who have said: "Lord, my refuge!"
and have made the Most High your dwelling.

Upon you no evil shall fall,
no plague approach where you dwell.
For you has he commanded his angels,
to keep you in all your ways.

They shall bear you upon their hands
lest you strike your foot against a stone.
On the lion and the viper you will tread
and trample the young lion and the dragon.

Since he clings to me in love, I will free him;
protect him for he knows my name.
When he calls I shall answer: "I am with you."
I will save him in distress and give him glory.

With length of life I will content him;
I shall let him see my saving power.

Glory to the Father, and to the Son,
and to the Holy Spirit:

as it was in the beginning, is now,
and will be forever. Amen.

Ant. Night holds no terrors for me sleeping under God's wings.

READING (Revelation 22:4-5)
They shall see the Lord face to face and bear his name on their foreheads. The night shall be no more. They will need no light from lamps or the sun, for the Lord God shall give them light, and they shall reign forever.

RESPONSORY
Into your hands, Lord, I commend my spirit.
– Into your hands, Lord, I commend my spirit.
You have redeemed us, Lord God of truth.
– I commend my spirit.
Glory to the Father, and to the Son, and to the Holy Spirit,
– Into your hands, Lord, I commend my spirit.

GOSPEL CANTICLE *(Luke 2:29-32)*
Christ is the light of the nations and the glory of Israel

Ant. Protect us, Lord, as we stay awake; watch over us as we sleep, that awake, we may keep watch with Christ, and asleep, rest in his peace.

Lord, † now you let your servant go in peace;
your word has been fulfilled:
my own eyes have seen the salvation
which you have prepared in the sight of every people: –

a light to reveal you to the nations
and the glory of your people Israel.

Glory to the Father, and to the Son,
and to the Holy Spirit:
as it was in the beginning, is now,
and will be forever. Amen.

Ant. Protect us, Lord, as we stay awake; watch over us as we sleep, that awake, we may keep watch with Christ, and asleep, rest in his peace.

CONCLUDING PRAYER

Lord, we have celebrated today
the mystery of the rising of Christ to new life.
May we now rest in your peace,
safe from all that could harm us,
and rise again refreshed and joyful,
to praise you throughout another day.
We ask this through Christ our Lord. Amen.

BLESSING

May † the all-powerful Lord grant us a restful night and a peaceful death. Amen.

MARIAN ANTIPHON (p. 84-87)

MONDAY

God, † come to my assistance.
– Lord, make haste to help me.

Glory to the Father, and to the Son, and to the Holy Spirit:
– as it was in the beginning, is now, and will be forever. Amen.
(Alleluia)

EXAMINATION OF CONSCIENCE

CONFITEOR (p. 17)

HYMN

PSALMODY

Ant. O Lord, our God, unwearied is your love for us.

Psalm 86 - Poor man's prayer in trouble
Blessed be God who comforts us in all our trials (2 Corinthians 1:3,4).

Turn your ear, O Lord, and give answer
for I am poor and needy.
Preserve my life, for I am faithful:
save the servant who trusts in you.

You are my God; have mercy on me, Lord,
for I cry to you all day long.
Give joy to your servant, O Lord,
for to you I lift up my soul.

O Lord, you are good and forgiving,
full of love to all who call.
Give heed, O Lord, to my prayer
and attend to the sound of my voice.

In the day of distress I will call
and surely you will reply.
Among the gods there is none like you, O Lord;
nor work to compare with yours.

All the nations shall come to adore you
and glorify your name, O Lord:
for you are great and do marvelous deeds,
you who alone are God.

Show me, Lord, your way
so that I may walk in your truth.
Guide my heart to fear your name.

I will praise you, Lord my God, with all my heart
and glorify your name forever;
for your love to me has been great:
you have saved me from the depths of the grave.

The proud have risen against me;
ruthless men seek my life;
to you they pay no heed.

But you, God of mercy and compassion,
slow to anger, O Lord,
abounding in love and truth,
turn and take pity on me.

O give your strength to your servant
and save your handmaid's son.
Show me a sign of your favor
that my foes may see to their shame
that you console me and give me your help.

Glory to the Father, and to the Son,
and to the Holy Spirit:

as it was in the beginning, is now,
and will be forever. Amen.

Ant. O Lord, our God, unwearied is your love for us.

READING (1 Thessalonians 5:9-10)
God has destined us for acquiring salvation through our Lord Jesus Christ. He died for us, that all of us, whether awake or asleep, together might live with him.

RESPONSORY
Into your hands, Lord, I commend my spirit.
– Into your hands, Lord, I commend my spirit.
You have redeemed us, Lord God of truth.
– I commend my spirit.
Glory to the Father, and to the Son, and to the Holy Spirit,
– Into your hands, Lord, I commend my spirit.

GOSPEL CANTICLE *(Luke 2:29-32)*
Christ is the light of the nations and the glory of Israel

Ant. Protect us, Lord, as we stay awake; watch over us as we sleep, that awake, we may keep watch with Christ, and asleep, rest in his peace.

Lord, † now you let your servant go in peace;
your word has been fulfilled:
my own eyes have seen the salvation
which you have prepared in the sight of every people:
a light to reveal you to the nations
and the glory of your people Israel.

Glory to the Father, and to the Son,
and to the Holy Spirit:
as it was in the beginning, is now,
and will be forever. Amen.

Ant. Protect us, Lord, as we stay awake; watch over us as we sleep, that awake, we may keep watch with Christ, and asleep, rest in his peace.

CONCLUDING PRAYER
Lord,
give our bodies restful sleep
and let the work we have done today
bear fruit in eternal life.
We ask this through Christ our Lord.
Amen.

BLESSING
May † the all-powerful Lord grant us a restful night and a peaceful death. Amen.

MARIAN ANTIPHON (p. 84-87)

TUESDAY

God, † come to my assistance.
– Lord, make haste to help me.

Glory to the Father, and to the Son, and to the Holy Spirit:
– as it was in the beginning, is now, and will be forever. Amen.
(Alleluia)

EXAMINATION OF CONSCIENCE

CONFITEOR (p. 17)

HYMN

PSALMODY

Ant. Do not hide your face from me; in you I put my trust.

Psalm 143 - Prayer in distress
Only by faith in Jesus Christ is a man made holy in God's sight. No observance of the law can achieve this (Galatians 2:16).

Lord, listen to my prayer:
turn your ear to my appeal.
You are faithful, you are just; give answer.
Do not call your servant to judgment
for no one is just in your sight.

The enemy pursues my soul;
he has crushed my life to the ground;
he has made me dwell in darkness
like the dead, long forgotten. –

Therefore my spirit fails;
my heart is numb within me.

I remember the days that are past:
I ponder all your works.
I muse on what your hand has wrought
and to you I stretch out my hands.
Like a parched land my soul thirsts for you.

Lord, make haste and answer;
for my spirit fails within me.
Do not hide your face
lest I become like those in the grave.

In the morning let me know your love
for I put my trust in you.
Make me know the way I should walk:
to you I lift up my soul.

Rescue me, Lord, from my enemies;
I have fled to you for refuge.
Teach me to do your will
for you, O Lord, are my God.
Let your good spirit guide me
in ways that are level and smooth.

For your name's sake, Lord, save my life;
in your justice save my soul from distress.

Glory to the Father, and to the Son,
and to the Holy Spirit

as it was in the beginning, is now,
and will be forever. Amen.

Ant. Do not hide your face from me; in you I put my trust.

READING (1 Peter 5:8-9a)
Stay sober and alert. Your opponent the devil is prowling like a roaring lion looking for someone to devour. Resist him, solid in your faith.

RESPONSORY
Into your hands, Lord, I commend my spirit.
– Into your hands, Lord, I commend my spirit.
You have redeemed us, Lord God of truth.
– I commend my spirit.
Glory to the Father, and to the Son, and to the Holy Spirit,
– Into your hands, Lord, I commend my spirit.

GOSPEL CANTICLE *(Luke 2:29-32)*
Christ is the light of the nations and the glory of Israel

Ant. Protect us, Lord, as we stay awake; watch over us as we sleep, that awake, we may keep watch with Christ, and asleep, rest in his peace.

Lord, † now you let your servant go in peace;
your word has been fulfilled:
my own eyes have seen the salvation
which you have prepared in the sight of every people:
a light to reveal you to the nations
and the glory of your people Israel.

Glory to the Father, and to the Son,
and to the Holy Spirit:
as it was in the beginning, is now,
and will be forever. Amen.

Ant. Protect us, Lord, as we stay awake; watch over us as we sleep, that awake, we may keep watch with Christ, and asleep, rest in his peace.

CONCLUDING PRAYER

Lord,
fill this night with your radiance.
May we sleep in peace and rise with joy
to welcome the light of a new day in your name.
We ask this through Christ our Lord.
Amen.

BLESSING

May † the all-powerful Lord grant us a restful night and a peaceful death. Amen.

MARIAN ANTIPHON (p. 84-87)

WEDNESDAY

God, † come to my assistance.
– Lord, make haste to help me.

Glory to the Father, and to the Son, and to the Holy Spirit:
– as it was in the beginning, is now, and will be forever. Amen.
(Alleluia)

EXAMINATION OF CONSCIENCE

CONFITEOR (p. 17)

HYMN

PSALMODY

Ant. Lord God, be my refuge and my strength.

Psalm 31:1-6 - Trustful prayer in adversity
Father, into your hands I commend my spirit (Luke 23:46).

In you, O Lord, I take refuge.
Let me never be put to shame.
In your justice, set me free,
hear me and speedily rescue me.

Be a rock of refuge for me,
a mighty stronghold to save me,
for you are my rock, my stronghold.
For your name's sake, lead me and guide me.

Release me from the snares they have hidden
for you are my refuge, Lord.
Into your hands I commend my spirit.
It is you who will redeem me, Lord.

Glory to the Father, and to the Son,
and to the Holy Spirit

as it was in the beginning, is now,
and will be forever. Amen.

Ant. Lord God, be my refuge and my strength.

Ant. 2 Out of the depths I cry to you, Lord.

Psalm 130 - A cry from the depths
He will save his people from their sins (Matthew 1:21).

Out of the depths I cry to you, O Lord,
Lord, hear my voice!
O let your ears be attentive
to the voice of my pleading.

If you, O Lord, should mark our guilt,
Lord, who would survive?
But with you is found forgiveness:
for this we revere you.

My soul is waiting for the Lord,
I count on his word.
My soul is longing for the Lord
more than watchman for daybreak.
Let the watchman count on daybreak
and Israel on the Lord.

Because with the Lord there is mercy
and fullness of redemption,
Israel indeed he will redeem
from all its iniquity.

Glory to the Father, and to the Son,
and to the Holy Spirit:

as it was in the beginning, is now,
and will be forever. Amen.

Ant. Out of the depths I cry to you, Lord.

READING (Ephesians 4:26-27)
If you are angry, let it be without sin. The sun must not go down on your wrath; do not give the devil a chance to work on you.

RESPONSORY
Into your hands, Lord, I commend my spirit.
– Into your hands, Lord, I commend my spirit.
You have redeemed us, Lord God of truth.
– I commend my spirit.
Glory to the Father, and to the Son, and to the Holy Spirit,
– Into your hands, Lord, I commend my spirit.

GOSPEL CANTICLE *(Luke 2:29-32)*
Christ is the light of the nations and the glory of Israel

Ant. Protect us, Lord, as we stay awake; watch over us as we sleep, that awake, we may keep watch with Christ, and asleep, rest in his peace.

Lord, † now you let your servant go in peace;
your word has been fulfilled:
my own eyes have seen the salvation
which you have prepared in the sight of every people:
a light to reveal you to the nations
and the glory of your people Israel.

Glory to the Father, and to the Son,
and to the Holy Spirit:
as it was in the beginning, is now,
and will be forever. Amen.

Ant. Protect us, Lord, as we stay awake; watch over us as we sleep, that awake, we may keep watch with Christ, and asleep, rest in his peace.

CONCLUDING PRAYER

Lord Jesus Christ,
you have given your followers
an example of gentleness and humility,
a task that is easy, a burden that is light.
Accept the prayers and work of this day,
and give us the rest that will strengthen us
to render more faithful service to you
who live and reign forever and ever.
Amen.

BLESSING

May † the all-powerful Lord grant us a restful night and a peaceful death. Amen.

MARIAN ANTIPHON (p. 84-87)

THURSDAY

God, † come to my assistance.
– Lord, make haste to help me.

Glory to the Father, and to the Son, and to the Holy Spirit:
– as it was in the beginning, is now, and will be forever. Amen.
(Alleluia)

EXAMINATION OF CONSCIENCE

CONFITEOR (p. 17)

HYMN

PSALMODY

Ant. In you, my God, my body will rest in hope.

Psalm 16 - God is my portion, my inheritance
The Father raised up Jesus from the dead and broke the bonds of death (Acts 2:24).

Preserve me, God, I take refuge in you.
I say to the Lord: "You are my God.
My happiness lies in you alone."

He has put into my heart a marvelous love
for the faithful ones who dwell in his land.
Those who choose other gods increase their sorrows.
Never will I offer their offerings of blood.
Never will I take their name upon my lips.

O Lord, it is you who are my portion and cup;
it is you yourself who are my prize.
The lot marked out for me is my delight:
welcome indeed the heritage that falls to me!

I will bless the Lord who gives me counsel,
who even at night directs my heart.
I keep the Lord ever in my sight:
since he is at my right hand, I shall stand firm.

And so my heart rejoices, my soul is glad;
even my body shall rest in safety.
For you will not leave my soul among the dead,
nor let your beloved know decay.

You will show me the path of life,
the fullness of joy in your presence,
at your right hand happiness forever.

Glory to the Father, and to the Son,
and to the Holy Spirit:

as it was in the beginning, is now,
and will be forever. Amen.

Ant. In you, my God, my body will rest in hope.

READING (1 Thessalonians 5:23)
May the God of peace make you perfect in holiness. May he preserve you whole and entire, spirit, soul, and body, irreproachable at the coming of our Lord Jesus Christ.

RESPONSORY

Into your hands, Lord, I commend my spirit.
– Into your hands, Lord, I commend my spirit.
You have redeemed us, Lord God of truth.
– I commend my spirit.
Glory to the Father, and to the Son, and to the Holy Spirit,
– Into your hands, Lord, I commend my spirit.

GOSPEL CANTICLE *(Luke 2:29-32)*

Christ is the light of the nations and the glory of Israel

Ant. Protect us, Lord, as we stay awake; watch over us as we sleep, that awake, we may keep watch with Christ, and asleep, rest in his peace.

Lord, † now you let your servant go in peace;
your word has been fulfilled:
my own eyes have seen the salvation
which you have prepared in the sight of every people:
a light to reveal you to the nations
and the glory of your people Israel.

Glory to the Father, and to the Son,
and to the Holy Spirit:
as it was in the beginning, is now,
and will be forever. Amen.

Ant. Protect us, Lord, as we stay awake; watch over us as we sleep, that awake, we may keep watch with Christ, and asleep, rest in his peace.

CONCLUDING PRAYER
Lord God,
send peaceful sleep
to refresh our tired bodies.
May your help always renew us
and keep us strong in your service.
We ask this through Christ our Lord.
Amen.

BLESSING
May † the all-powerful Lord grant us a restful night and a peaceful death. Amen.

MARIAN ANTIPHON (p. 84-87)

FRIDAY

God, † come to my assistance.
– Lord, make haste to help me.

Glory to the Father, and to the Son, and to the Holy Spirit:
– as it was in the beginning, is now, and will be forever. Amen.
(Alleluia)

EXAMINATION OF CONSCIENCE

CONFITEOR (p. 17)

HYMN

PSALMODY

Ant. Day and night I cry to you, my God.

Psalm 88 - Prayer of a sick person
This is your hour when darkness reigns (Luke 22:53).

Lord my God, I call for help by day;
I cry at night before you.
Let my prayer come into your presence.
O turn your ear to my cry.

For my soul is filled with evils;
my life is on the brink of the grave.
I am reckoned as one in the tomb:
I have reached the end of my strength,

like one alone among the dead;
like the slain lying in their graves;
like those you remember no more,
cut off, as they are, from your hand.

You have laid me in the depths of the tomb,
in places that are dark, in the depths.
Your anger weighs down upon me:
I am drowned beneath your waves.

You have taken away my friends
and made me hateful in their sight.
Imprisoned, I cannot escape;
my eyes are sunken with grief.

I call to you, Lord, all the day long;
to you I stretch out my hands. –

Will you work your wonders for the dead?
Will the shades stand and praise you?

Will your love be told in the grave
or your faithfulness among the dead?
Will your wonders be known in the dark
or your justice in the land of oblivion?

As for me, Lord, I call to you for help:
in the morning my prayer comes before you.
Lord, why do you reject me?
Why do you hide your face?

Wretched, close to death from my youth,
I have borne your trials; I am numb.
Your fury has swept down upon me;
your terrors have utterly destroyed me.

They surround me all the day like a flood,
they assail me all together.
Friend and neighbor you have taken away:
my one companion is darkness.

Glory to the Father, and to the Son,
and to the Holy Spirit:

as it was in the beginning, is now,
and will be forever. Amen.

Ant. Day and night I cry to you, my God.

READING (Jeremiah 14:9a)
You are in our midst, O Lord,
your name we bear:
do not forsake us, O Lord, our God!

RESPONSORY
Into your hands, Lord, I commend my spirit.
– Into your hands, Lord, I commend my spirit.
You have redeemed us, Lord God of truth.
– I commend my spirit.
Glory to the Father, and to the Son, and to the Holy Spirit,
– Into your hands, Lord, I commend my spirit.

GOSPEL CANTICLE *(Luke 2:29-32)*
Christ is the light of the nations and the glory of Israel

Ant. Protect us, Lord, as we stay awake; watch over us as we sleep, that awake, we may keep watch with Christ, and asleep, rest in his peace.

Lord, † now you let your servant go in peace;
your word has been fulfilled:
my own eyes have seen the salvation
which you have prepared in the sight of every people:
a light to reveal you to the nations
and the glory of your people Israel.

Glory to the Father, and to the Son,
and to the Holy Spirit:
as it was in the beginning, is now,
and will be forever. Amen.

Ant. Protect us, Lord, as we stay awake; watch over us as we sleep, that awake, we may keep watch with Christ, and asleep, rest in his peace.

CONCLUDING PRAYER

All-powerful God,
keep us united with your Son
in his death and burial
so that we may rise to new life with him,
who lives and reigns forever and ever. Amen.

BLESSING

May † the all-powerful Lord grant us a restful night and a peaceful death. Amen.

MARIAN ANTIPHON (p. 84-87)

SATURDAY

God, † come to my assistance.
– Lord, make haste to help me.

Glory to the Father, and to the Son, and to the Holy Spirit:
– as it was in the beginning, is now, and will be forever. Amen. (Alleluia)

EXAMINATION OF CONSCIENCE

CONFITEOR (p. 17)

HYMN

PSALMODY

Ant. Have mercy, Lord, and hear my prayer.

Psalm 4 - Thanksgiving

The resurrection of Christ was God's supreme and wholly marvelous work (St. Augustine).

When I call, answer me, O God of justice;
from anguish you released me; have mercy and hear me!

O men, how long will your hearts be closed,
will you love what is futile and seek what is false?

It is the Lord who grants favors to those whom he loves;
the Lord hears me whenever I call him.

Fear him; do not sin: ponder on your bed and be still.
Make justice your sacrifice and trust in the Lord.

"What can bring us happiness?" many say.
Let the light of your face shine on us, O Lord.

You have put into my heart a greater joy
than they have from abundance of corn and new wine.

I will lie down in peace and sleep comes at once
for you alone, Lord, make me dwell in safety.

Glory to the Father, and to the Son,
and to the Holy Spirit

as it was in the beginning, is now,
and will be forever. Amen.

Ant. Have mercy, Lord, and hear my prayer.

Ant. 2 In the silent hours of night, bless the Lord.

Psalm 134 - Evening prayer in the temple
Praise our God, all you his servants, you who fear him, small and great (Revelation 19:5).

O come, bless the Lord,
all you who serve the Lord,
who stand in the house of the Lord,
in the courts of the house of our God.

Lift up your hands to the holy place
and bless the Lord through the night.

May the Lord bless you from Zion,
he who made both heaven and earth.

Glory to the Father, and to the Son,
and to the Holy Spirit:

as it was in the beginning, is now,
and will be forever. Amen.

Ant. In the silent hours of night, bless the Lord.

READING (Deuteronomy 6:4-7)
Hear, O Israel! The Lord is our God, the Lord alone! Therefore, you shall love the Lord, your God, with all your heart, and with all your soul, and with all your strength. Take to heart these words which I enjoin on you today. Drill them into your children. Speak of them at home and abroad, whether you are busy or at rest.

RESPONSORY

Into your hands, Lord, I commend my spirit.
– Into your hands, Lord, I commend my spirit.
You have redeemed us, Lord God of truth.
– I commend my spirit.
Glory to the Father, and to the Son, and to the Holy Spirit,
– Into your hands, Lord, I commend my spirit.

GOSPEL CANTICLE *(Luke 2:29-32)*

Christ is the light of the nations and the glory of Israel

Ant. Protect us, Lord, as we stay awake; watch over us as we sleep, that awake, we may keep watch with Christ, and asleep, rest in his peace.

Lord, † now you let your servant go in peace;
your word has been fulfilled:
my own eyes have seen the salvation
which you have prepared in the sight of every people:
a light to reveal you to the nations
and the glory of your people Israel.

Glory to the Father, and to the Son,
and to the Holy Spirit:
as it was in the beginning, is now,
and will be forever. Amen.

Ant. Protect us, Lord, as we stay awake; watch over us as we sleep, that awake, we may keep watch with Christ, and asleep, rest in his peace.

CONCLUDING PRAYER

Lord, be with us throughout this night.
When day comes may we rise from sleep
to rejoice in the resurrection of your Christ,
who lives and reigns forever and ever. Amen.

BLESSING

May † the all-powerful Lord grant us a restful night and a peaceful death. Amen.

MARIAN ANTIPHON (p. 84-87)

HYMNS

Like the inspired writers
of the New Testament,
the first Christian communities
read the Book of Psalms in a new way,
singing in it the mystery of Christ.
In the newness of the Spirit,
they also composed hymns and canticles
in the light of the unheard-of event
that God accomplished in his Son:
his Incarnation, his death
which conquered death, his Resurrection,
and Ascension to the right hand of the Father.[1]

Catechism of the Catholic Church (¶ 2641)

[1] *Cf. Phil 2:6-11; Col 1:15-20; Eph 5:14; 1 Tim 3:16; 6:15-16; 2 Tim 2:11-13.*

**All hymns are Public Domain unless otherwise noted.*

All Creatures

St. Francis of Assisi (1181-1226)
trans. William H. Draper (1855-1933)

All creatures of our God and King
Lift up your voice and hear us sing
O praise Him, alleluia!
Thou burning sun with golden beam
Thou silver moon with softer gleam

O praise Him, O praise Him
Alleluia, alleluia, alleluia!

Thou rushing wind that art so strong
Ye clouds that sail in heaven along
O praise Him, alleluia!
Thou rising morn in praise rejoice
Ye lights of evening find a voice

O praise Him, O praise Him
Alleluia, alleluia, alleluia!

Let all things their Creator bless
And worship Him in humbleness
O praise Him, alleluia!
Praise, praise the Father, praise the Son
And praise the Spirit, Three in One

O praise Him, O praise Him
Alleluia, alleluia, alleluia!

Ave Maris Stella

St. Venantius Fortunatus (530-609)
arr. Colleen Nixon (1985-)

Hail, bright star of ocean
God's own Mother blest
Ever sinless Virgin
Gate of heavenly rest
Taking that sweet Ave
Which from Gabriel came
Peace confirm within us
Changing Eva's name

Break the captives' fetters
Light on blindness pour
All our ills expelling
Every bliss implore
Show thyself a Mother
May the Word Divine
Born for us thy Infant
Hear our prayers through thine

Ave Maris Stella (3x)
Ave

Virgin all excelling
Mildest of the mild
Freed from guilt preserve us
Pure and undefiled –

Keep our life all spotless
Make our way secure
Till we find in Jesus
Joy forevermore

Ave Maris Stella (3x)
Ave

Through the highest heaven
To the Almighty Three
Father, Son and Spirit
One same glory be
One same glory be
One same glory be
Glory be to God

Ave Maris Stella (3x)
Ave

Be Thou My Vision

att. St. Dallan Forgaill (530-598)
trans. Mary E. Byrne, (1880-1931)

Be Thou my Vision O Lord of my heart
Naught be all else to me save that Thou art
Thou my best Thought by day or by night
Waking or sleeping Thy presence my light

Be Thou my Wisdom and Thou my true Word
I ever with Thee and Thou with me, Lord
Thou my great Father and I Thy true son
Thou in me dwelling and I with Thee one

Riches I heed not nor man's empty praise
Thou mine inheritance now and always
Thou and Thou only first in my heart
High King of Heaven my Treasure Thou art

High King of Heaven my victory won
May I reach Heaven's joys O bright Heaven's Sun
Heart of my own heart whatever befall
Still be my Vision O Ruler of all

Behold the Mystery

St. Thomas Aquinas (1227-1274)
trans. Fr. John M. Neale (1818-1866)
ref. & arr. Colleen Nixon (1985-) & Jimmy Mitchell (1985-)

Of the glorious Body telling
O my tongue its mysteries sing
And the Blood all price excelling
Which the world's eternal King
In a noble womb once dwelling
Shed for the world's ransoming

Word made Flesh by word He maketh
Very bread his Flesh to be
Man in wine Christ's Blood partaketh
And if senses fail to see
Faith alone the true heart waketh
To behold the mystery

Our hope is here, Mary's Son
Come adore Him
Behold the Mystery
Three in One, Trinity
Praise God, true Love made flesh
Here in Word and Sacrament

Therefore we before Him bending
This great Sacrament revere
Types and shadows have their ending
For the newer rite is here
Faith our outward sense befriending
Makes the inward vision clear

Glory let us give and blessing
To the Father and Son
Honor and might praise addressing
While eternal ages run
Ever to His love confessing
With the Holy Spirit, come!

Behold He's here, behold He's here
The Myst'ry of Love
Behold He's here, behold He's here
God-with-us

Christe Qui Splendor

From the Liturgia Horarum (ca. 8th cent.)

Christe qui splendor et dies
noctis tenebras detegis,
lucisque lumen crederis,
lumen beatis praedicans,

Precamur, sancte Domine,
hac nocte nos custodias;
sit nobis in te requies,
quietas horas tribue.

Somno si dantur oculi,
cor semper ad te vigilet;
tuaque dextra protegas
fideles, qui te diligunt.

Defensor noster, aspice,
insidiantes reprime,
guberna tuos famulos,
quos sanguine mercatus es.

Sit, Christe, rex piissime,
tibi Patrique gloria,
cum Spiritu Paraclito,
in sempiterna saecula.
Amen.

Come Holy Ghost

Rhabanus Maurus (776-856)
trans. Richard Mant (1776-1848)

Come Holy Ghost, Creator blest
And in our souls take up Thy rest
Come with Thy grace and heavenly aid
To fill the hearts which Thou hast made (2x)

To Thee the Comforter, we cry
To Thee the Gift of God most high
The Fount of life, the Fire of love
The soul's anointing from above (2x)

O Finger of the hand divine
The sevenfold gifts of grace are Thine
True promise of the Father Thou
Who dost the tongue with power endow (2x)

Thy light to every sense impart
And shed Thy love in every heart
Thine own unfailing might supply
To strengthen our infirmity (2x)

Praise be to Thee, Father and Son
And Holy Spirit, Three in One
And may the Son on us bestow
The gifts that from the Spirit flow (2x)

Come Thou Fount

Robert Robinson (1735-1790)

Come Thou fount of every blessing
Tune my heart to sing Thy grace
Streams of mercy never ceasing
Call for songs of loudest praise
Teach me some melodious sonnet
Sung by flaming tongues above
Praise the mount I'm fixed upon it
Mount of Thy redeeming love

Here I raise my heart to Thee Lord
Here by Thy great help I've come
And I hope by Thy good pleasure
Safely to arrive at home
Jesus sought me when a stranger
Wandering from the fold of God
He to rescue me from danger
Interposed His precious blood

O to grace how great a debtor
Daily I'm constrained to be
Let Thy goodness like a fetter
Bind my wandering heart to Thee
Prone to wander, Lord I feel it
Prone to leave the God I love
Here's my heart, O take and seal it
Seal it for Thy courts above

Consumed By Grace

v. 1, St. Teresa of Avila (1515-1582); arr., vv. 2-3, & ref., Colleen Nixon

Let nothing disturb you, let nothing affright you
All things are passing, God never changes
Patient endurance obtains all it strives for
With God as your portion, nothing is wanting
Alone God suffices

Alone, You are enough
God, You are all we need
And with You we plead, consume us alone
You are the King,
And though we crowned You with thorns
You crown us with glory, humbly we thank You

Consumed by grace, consumed by grace
Consumed Lord, consumed by Your grace
Consumed by grace, consumed by grace
God we are unworthy, still You embrace
And consume us with grace

Alone, You are the Lamb
The Lamb of God and calling
Calling us to Your Table
To consume you alone
You are the Bread
You are the wine we are drinking
Give us the faith to see You
When our human sense is failing

Creator of the Stars

John M. Neale, Colleen Nixon, & Jimmy Mitchell

Grieving that the ancient curse
Should doom to death a universe
You sent the remedy of grace
To save and heal a wounded race
You came the Bridegroom of the Bride
As drew the world to eveningtide
Proceeding from a Virgin shrine
The spotless Victim all divine

Creator of the stars of night
Our everlasting light
Redeeming One who saves us all
Here us as we call

To Your sweet Name majestic now
All knees must bend, all hearts must bow
And things in Heaven You shall own
And all on earth the Lord alone
To God the Father, God the Son,
And God the Spirit, Three in One,
Laud, honor, might, and glory be
From age to age eternally.

Come Emmanuel, pierce the sorrows of our soul
Be our hope when shadows rise
Be our strength in darkest night
Be Emmanuel

Doxology

Thomas Ken (1637-1711)

Praise God from Whom all blessings flow
Praise Him all creatures here below
Praise Him above ye heavenly host
Praise Father, Son, and Holy Ghost

Faith of our Fathers

Fr. Frederick W. Faber (1814-1863)

Faith of our fathers living still
In spite of dungeon fire and sword
O how our hearts beat high with joy
Whenever we hear that glorious Word

Faith of our fathers, holy faith
We will be true to thee till death

Faith of our fathers, we will love
Both friend and foe in all our strife
And preach Thee, too, as love knows how
By kindly words and virtuous life

Faith of our fathers, Mary's prayers
Shall win all nations unto Thee
And through the truth that comes from God
We all shall then be truly free

Fairest Lord Jesus

anon., "Schönster Herr Jesu," ca. 1662
trans. Joseph A. Seiss (1823-1904)

Fairest Lord Jesus, Ruler of all nature
O Thou of God and man the Son
Thee will I cherish, Thee will I honor
Thou my soul's glory, joy, and crown

Fair are the meadows, fairer still the woodlands,
Robed in the blooming garb of spring
Jesus is fairer, Jesus is purer
Who makes the woeful heart to sing

Fair is the sunshine, fairer still the moonlight
And all the twinkling starry host
Jesus shines brighter, Jesus shines purer
Than all the angels heaven can boast

Beautiful Savior! Lord of all the nations!
Son of God and Son of Man!
Glory and honor, praise, adoration
Now and forever more be Thine

Firmly I Believe

Bl. John Henry Newman (1801-1890)
arr. Jimmy Mitchell (1985-)

Firmly I believe and truly
God is Three, and God is One
And I next acknowledge duly
Manhood taken by the Son
And I trust and hope most fully
In that Manhood crucified
And each thought and deed unruly
Do to death, as He has died

Adoration e'er be given,
With and through the angelic host
To the God of earth and Heaven
Father, Son and Holy Ghost

Simply to His grace and wholly
Light and life and strength belong
And I love supremely, solely
Him the holy, Him the strong
And I hold in veneration
For the love of Him alone
Holy Church as His creation
And her teachings are His own

And I take with joy whatever
Now besets me, pain or fear
And with a strong will I sever
All the ties which bind me here

Give Me Jesus

trad. American hymn (ca. 19th cent.)

In the morning, when I rise
In the morning, when I rise
In the morning, when I rise
Give me Jesus

Give me Jesus
Give me Jesus
You can have all this world
Just give me Jesus

When I am alone
When I am alone
When I am alone
Give me Jesus

When I come to die
When I come to die
When I come to die
Give me Jesus

Hail Holy Queen

trans. anon. from "Roman Hymnal" (ca. 1884)

Hail, holy Queen enthroned above, O Maria
Hail, Queen of mercy and of love, O Maria

Triumph, all ye cherubim
Sing with us, ye seraphim
Heaven and earth resound the hymn
Salve, salve, salve Regina!

Our life, our sweetness, here below, O Maria
Our hope in sorrow and in woe, O Maria

To thee we cry, poor sons of Eve, O Maria
To thee we sigh, we mourn, we grieve, O Maria

Turn then most gracious Advocate, O Maria
Toward us thine eyes compassionate, O Maria

The cause of joy to men below, O Maria
The spring through which all graces flow, O Maria

Heaven's Before Me

Pope John XXII (1249-1334)
ref. & arr. Colleen Nixon (1985-)

Soul of Christ, sanctify me
Body of Christ, save me please
Blood of Christ, inebriate me
And with the water of Your side, Lord
Wash me clean
Passion of Christ, strengthen me
And oh good Jesus, hear my plea

'Cause Heaven's before me (repeat)

Within Thy wounds, will you hide me
Suffer me not separation from Thee
From the enemy, oh Father
Please defend me
And at the hour of my death, God
Call me Home
And bid me come unto Thee
So with Your saints I may praise Thee
With all angels I may praise Thee

Incline my heart to do Your will
My heart is Thine (repeat)

Holy, Holy, Holy

Reginald Herber (1783-1826)

Holy, holy, holy! Lord God Almighty!
Early in the morning our song shall rise to Thee
Holy, holy, holy, merciful and mighty!
God in three Persons, blessed Trinity!

Holy, holy, holy! All the saints adore Thee
Casting down their golden crowns around the glassy sea
Cherubim and seraphim, falling down before Thee
Who was, and is, and evermore shall be

Holy, holy, holy! Though the darkness hide Thee
Though the eye of sinful man Thy glory may not see
Only Thou art holy; there is none beside Thee
Perfect in power, in love, and purity

Holy, holy, holy! Lord God Almighty!
All Thy works shall praise Thy Name
In earth, and sky, and sea
Holy, holy, holy; merciful and mighty!
God in three Persons, blessed Trinity!

Holy God

metrical "Te Deum", att. Fr. Ignaz Franz (1719-1790)
trans. C. A. Walworth (1820-1900)

Holy God, we praise Thy Name
Lord of all, we bow before Thee!
All on earth Thy scepter claim
All in Heaven above adore Thee
Infinite Thy vast domain
Everlasting is Thy reign

Hark! the loud celestial hymn
Angel choirs above are raising
Cherubim and seraphim
In unceasing chorus praising
Fill the heavens with sweet accord
Holy, holy, holy, Lord

Holy Father, Holy Son
Holy Spirit, Three we name Thee
While in essence only One
Undivided God we claim Thee
And adoring bend the knee
While we own the mystery

How Marvelous (I Stand Amazed)

Charles H. Gabriel (1856-1932)

I stand amazed in the presence of
Jesus the Nazarene
And wonder how He could love me
A sinner, so wounded, unclean
He took my sins and my sorrows
He made them his very own
And bore the burden to Calvary
And suffered and died alone

How marvelous! How wonderful!
E'er my song shall ever be
How marvelous! How wonderful
Is my Savior's love for me

For me it was in the garden
He prayed: "Not my will, but thine."
He had no tears for His own griefs
but sweat-drops of blood for mine
In pity angels beheld Him
And came from the world of light
To comfort Him in the sorrows
He bore for my soul that night

When with the ransomed in all their glory
His face at last I'll see
'Twill be my joy through the ages
To sing of His love for me

I Heard the Voice

Horatius Bonar (1808-1889)

I heard the voice of Jesus say
"Come unto me and rest
Lay down, thou weary one, lay down
Thy head upon my breast"
I came to Jesus as I was
So weary, worn, and sad
I found in Him a resting place
And He has made me glad

I heard the voice of Jesus say
"Behold, I freely give
The living water, thirsty one
Stoop down and drink and live"
I came to Jesus, and I drank
Of that life-giving stream
My thirst was quenched, my soul revived
And now I live in Him

I heard the voice of Jesus say,
"I am this dark world's light;
look unto me, thy morn shall rise,
and all thy day be bright."
I looked to Jesus, and I found
in Him my Star, my Sun;
and in that light of life I'll walk
till traveling days are done.

Immaculate Mary

Fr. Jeremiah W. Cummings (1814-1866)
alt. ref. anon., ca. 1897

Immaculate Mary, thy praises we sing
Who reignest in splendor with Jesus our King

Ave, Ave, Ave, Maria! (repeat)

In Heaven the blessed thy glory proclaim
On earth we thy children invoke thy fair name

We pray for God's glory, may His kingdom come
We pray for His Vicar, our Father in Rome

We pray for our Mother, the Church upon earth
And bless, dearest Lady, the land of our birth

It Is Well

Horatio G. Spafford (1828-1888)

When peace, like a river, attendeth my way
When sorrow like sea billows roll
Whatever the cost, Thou has taught me to say
It is well, it is well, with my soul

It is well, with my soul
It is well, it is well, with my soul

My sin, oh the bliss, of this glorious thought
My sin, not in part, but the whole
Is nailed to the cross and I bear it no more
Praise the Lord, praise the Lord, oh my soul

It is well, with my soul
It is well, it is well, with my soul

And Lord, haste the day when my faith shall be sight
The clouds be rolled back as a scroll
The trump shall resound and the Lord shall descend
Even so, it is well with my soul

Joyful, Joyful

Henry Van Dyke, Ludwig van Beethoven, & Edward Hodges

Joyful, joyful, we adore Thee
God of glory, Lord of love
Hearts unfold like flowers before Thee
Opening to the sun above
Melt the clouds of sin and sadness
Drive the dark of doubt away
Giver of immortal gladness
Fill us with the light of day

All Thy works with joy surround Thee
Earth and heaven reflect Thy rays
Stars and angels sing around Thee
Center of unbroken praise
Field and forest, vale and mountain
Flowery meadow, flashing sea
Chanting bird and flowing fountain
Call us to rejoice in Thee

Thou art giving and forgiving
Ever blessing, ever blest
Well-spring of the joy of living
Ocean depth of happy rest
Thou our Father, Christ our brother
All who live in love are Thine
Teach us how to love each other
Lift us to the joy divine

King of Love

Henry W. Baker (1821-1877)

The King of love my shepherd is
Whose goodness faileth never
I nothing lack if I am His
And He is mine forever

Where streams of living water flow
My ransomed soul He leadeth
And, where the verdant pastures grow
With food celestial feedeth

Perverse and foolish oft I strayed
But yet in love He sought me
And on His shoulder gently laid
And home rejoicing brought me

In death's dark vale I fear no ill
With Thee, dear Lord, beside me
Thy rod and staff my comfort still
Thy cross before to guide me

Thou spread'st a table in my sight
Thine unction grace bestoweth
And, oh, what transport of delight
From Thy pure chalice floweth

And so through all the length of days
Thy goodness faileth never
Good Shepherd, may I sing Thy praise
Within Thy house forever

Lead Kindly Light

vv. 1-3, Bl. J.H. Newman (1801-1890)
v. 4, E. H. Bickersteth, Jr. (1825-1906)

Lead, kindly Light, amid th'encircling gloom
Lead Thou me on
The night is dark, and I am far from home
Lead Thou me on
Keep Thou my feet; I do not ask to see
The distant scene; one step enough for me

I was not ever thus, nor prayed that Thou
Shouldst lead me on
I loved to choose and see my path but now
Lead Thou me on
I loved the garish day, and, spite of fears
Pride ruled my will; remember not past years

So long Thy power hath blest me sure it still
Will lead me on
O'er moor and fen, o'er crag and torrent 'till
The night is gone
And with the morn those angel faces smile
Which I have loved, long since and lost awhile

Meantime, along the narrow rugged path
Thyself hast trod
Lead, Savior, lead me home in childlike faith
Home to my God
To rest forever after earthly strife
In the calm light of everlasting life

Let All Mortal Flesh

Liturgy of St. James (ca. 4th cent.)
trans. Gerard Moultrie (1829-1885)

Let all mortal flesh keep silence,
And with fear and trembling stand;
Ponder nothing earthly minded,
For with blessing in His hand,
Christ our God to earth descendeth,
Our full homage to demand.

King of kings, yet born of Mary,
As of old on earth He stood,
Lord of lords, in human vesture,
In the body and the blood;
He will give to all the faithful
His own self for heavenly food.

Rank on rank the host of heaven
Spreads its vanguard on the way,
As the Light of light descendeth
From the realms of endless day,
That the powers of hell may vanish
As the darkness clears away.

At His feet the six wingèd seraph,
Cherubim with sleepless eye,
Veil their faces to the presence,
As with ceaseless voice they cry:
Alleluia, Alleluia
Alleluia, Lord Most High!

O Bread of Heaven

St. Alphonsus Liguori (1696-1787)
trans. Robert A. Coffin (1819-1885)

O Bread of Heaven, beneath this veil
Thou dost my very God conceal
My Jesus, dearest treasure, hail!
I love Thee and, adoring, kneel
Each loving soul by Thee is fed
With Thine own Self in form of Bread

O food of life, Thou Who dost give
The pledge of immortality
I live, no 'tis not I that live
God gives me life, God lives in me
He feeds my soul, He guides my ways
And every grief with joy repays

O Bond of love that dost unite
The servant to his living Lord
Could I dare live and not requite
Such love - then death were meet reward
I cannot live unless to prove
Some love for such unmeasured love

Beloved Lord, in Heaven above
There, Jesus, Thou awaitest me
To gaze on Thee with endless love
Yes, thus I hope, thus shall it be
For how can He deny me Heaven
Who here on earth Himself hath given?

O Christ Who Is the Light

Christe Qui Splendor (Liturgia Horarum, ca. 8th cent.)
trans. Wiliiam J. Copeland (1804-1885)

O Christ, who is the Light and Day
Thou drivest darksome night away!
We know Thee as the Light of light
Illuminating mortal sight.

All holy Lord, we pray to Thee
Keep us tonight from danger free
Grant us, dear Lord, in Thee to rest
So be our sleep in quiet blest.

And while the eyes soft slumber take
Still be the heart to Thee awake
Be Thy right hand upheld above
Thy servants resting in Thy love.

Yea, our Defender, be Thou nigh
To bid the powers of darkness fly
Keep us from sin, and guide for good
Thy servants purchased by Thy blood.

Remember us, dear Lord, we pray
While in this mortal flesh we stay
'Tis Thou who dost the soul defend
Be present with us to the end.

Blest Three in One and One in Three
Almighty God, we pray to Thee
That Thou wouldst now vouchsafe to bless
Our fast with fruits of righteousness. Amen.

O Holy Spirit

Désiré-Joseph Cardinal Mercier (1851-1926)
trans. Anon. (ca. 20th cent.)

O Holy Spirit, beloved of my soul, I adore You
Enlighten me, guide me
Strengthen me, console me
Tell me what I should do; give me Your orders
I promise to submit myself
To all that You desire of me
And to accept all that You permit
To happen to me
Let me only know Your Will

O Sacrament Most Holy

ca. 1777, trans. Anon. (ca. 19th cent.)
ref. & arr. Colleen Nixon (1985-) © 2011 Mysterium

O Lord, I am not worthy
That Thou should'st come to me
But speak the words of comfort
My spirit healed shall be
O Jesus, we adore Thee
Our Victim and our Priest
Whose precious Blood and Body
Become our sacred Feast

O Sacrament most holy
O Sacrament divine
All praise and all thanksgiving
Be ev'ry moment Thine

Increase my faith, dear Jesus
In Thy real Presence here
Prepare me to receive Thee
Into my heart draw near
And humbly I'll receive Thee
The Bridegroom of my soul
No more by sin to grieve Thee
Or fly Thy sweet control

Mercy and grace flow from Your side

O come, all you who labor
In sorrow and in pain
Come, eat This Bread from heaven
Thy peace and strength regain

O Sacred Head

St. Bernard of Clairvaux (1090-1153)
trans. H.W. Baker (1821-1877)

O sacred head, surrounded
By crown of piercing thorn!
O bleeding head, so wounded
Reviled and put to scorn!
Our sins have marred the glory
Of Thy most holy face
Yet angel hosts adore Thee
And tremble as they gaze

I see Thy strength and vigor
All fading in the strife
And death with cruel rigor
Bereaving Thee of life
O agony and dying!
O love to sinners free!
Jesus, all grace supplying
O turn Thy face on me

In this Thy bitter passion
Good Shepherd, think of me
With Thy most sweet compassion
Unworthy though I be
Beneath Thy cross abiding
For ever would I rest
In Thy dear love confiding
And with Thy presence blest

O Worship the King

Robert Grant (1779-1838) & Johann Michael Haydn (1737-1806)

O worship the King, all glorious above
O gratefully sing God's power and God's love
Our Shield and Defender, the Ancient of Days
Pavilioned in splendor, and girded with praise

O tell of God's might, O sing of God's grace
Whose robe is the light, whose canopy space
Whose chariots of wrath the deep thunderclouds form
And dark is God's path on the wings of the storm

The earth with its store of wonders untold
Almighty, thy power hath founded of old
Hath 'stablished it fast by a changeless decree
And round it hath cast, like a mantle, the sea

Thy bountiful care, what tongue can recite
It breathes in the air, it shines in the light
It streams from the hills, it descends to the plain
And sweetly distills in the dew and the rain

Frail children of dust, and feeble as frail
In thee do we trust, nor find thee to fail
Thy mercies how tender, how firm to the end
Our Maker, Defender, Redeemer, and Friend

Praise to the Lord

Joachim Neander (1650-1680)
trans. Catherine Winkworth (1827-1878)

Praise to the Lord, the Almighty
The King of creation!
O my soul, praise Him
For He is thy health and salvation!
All ye who hear, now to His temple draw near
Praise Him in glad adoration

Praise to the Lord, who o'er all things
So wondrously reigneth
Shelters thee under His wings
Yea, so gently sustaineth!
Hast thou not seen, how thy desires e'er have been
Granted in what He ordaineth?

Praise to the Lord, who doth prosper
Thy work and defend thee
Surely His goodness and mercy
Here daily attend thee.
Ponder anew what the Almighty can do,
If with His love He befriend thee.

Praise to the Lord
O let all that is in me adore Him!
All that hath life and breath
Come now with praises before Him
Let the Amen sound from His people again
Gladly for e'er we adore Him

Sing of Mary

Roland F. Palmer (1898-1978)

Sing of Mary, pure and lowly
Virgin Mother undefiled
Sing of God's own Son most holy
Who became her little Child
Fairest Child of fairest mother
God the Lord who came to earth
Word made flesh, our very Brother
Takes our nature by His birth

Sing of Jesus, son of Mary
In the home at Nazareth
Toil and labor cannot weary
Love enduring unto death
Constant was the love He gave her
Though He went forth from her side
Forth to preach and heal and suffer
Till on Calvary He died

Sing of Mary, sing of Jesus
Holy Mother's holier Son
From His throne in heav'n He sees us
There He calls ev'ry one
Where He welcomes home His Mother
To a place at His right hand
There His faithful servants gather
There the crowned victors stand

Joyful Mother, full of gladness
In Thine arms thy Lord was borne –

Mournful Mother, full of sadness
All thy heart with pain was torn
Glorious Mother, now rewarded
With a crown at Jesus' hand,
Age to age thy name recorded
Shall be blest in ev'ry land

Glory be to God the Father
Glory be to God the Son
Glory be to God the Spirit
Glory to the Three in One
From the heart of blessed Mary
From all Saints the song ascends
And the Church the strain reechoes
Unto earth's remotest ends

Sweet Sacrament

Fr. Frederick W. Faber (1814-1863)

Jesus, my Lord, my God, my all
How can I love Thee as I ought?
And how revere this wond'rous gift
So far surpassing hope or thought?

Had I but Mary's sinless heart
To love Thee with, my dearest King
O with what bursts of fervent praise
Thy goodness, Jesus, would I sing!

Sweet Sacrament, we Thee adore
O make us love Thee more and more!
O make us love Thee more and more!

O, see, within a creature's hand
The vast Creator deigns to be
Reposing infant-like, as though
On Joseph's arm, on Mary's knee

Thy body, soul, and Godhead, all
O Mystery of Love divine!
I cannot compass all I have
For all Thou hast and art are mine

Sound His praises higher still
And come ye Angels to our aid
'Tis God, 'tis God, the very God
Whose power both man and angels made

Take My Life

Frances R. Haverhill (1836-1879)

Take my life, and let it be
Consecrated, Lord, to Thee
Take my moments and my days
Let them flow in ceaseless praise

Take my hands, and let them move
At the impulse of Thy love
Take my feet and let them be
Swift and beautiful for Thee

Take my voice, and let me sing
Always, only, for my King
Take my lips, and let them be
Filled with messages from Thee

Take my silver and my gold
Not a mite would I withhold
Take my intellect, and use
Every power as Thou shalt choose

Take my will, and make it Thine
It shall be no longer mine
Take my heart; it is Thine own
It shall be Thy royal throne

Take my love; my Lord, I pour
At Thy feet its treasure-store
Take myself, and I will be
Ever, only, all for Thee

Te Lucis

trans. J.M. Neale (1818-1866)
Latin ca. 7th cent.

To Thee, before the close of day
Creator of the world, we pray
That with Thy wonted favor, Thou
Wouldst be our Guard and Keeper now.

From all ill dreams defend our eyes
From nightly fears and fantasies
Tread under foot our ghostly foe
That no pollution we may know.

O Father, that we ask be done
Through Jesus Christ Thine only Son
Who, with the Holy Ghost and Thee
Shall live and reign eternally. Amen.

Te lucis ante términum,
rerum Creátor, póscimus,
ut sólita cleméntia
sis præsul ad custódiam.

Procul recédant sómnia
et nóctium phantásmata;
hostémque nostrum cómprime,
ne polluántur córpora.

Præsta, Pater omnípotens,
per Iesum Christum Dóminum,
qui tecum in perpétuum
regnat cum Sancto Spíritu. Amen.

Turn Your Eyes

Helen H. Lemmel (1863-1961)
alt. vv. 2 & 3, Dillon E. Barker (1983-)

O soul, are you weary and troubled?
No light in the darkness you see?
There's a light for a look at the Savior
And life more abundant and free!

Turn your eyes upon Jesus
Look full in His wonderful face
And the things of earth
Will grow strangely dim
In the light of His glory and grace

Through death into life everlasting
He passed, and we hope to go there
Through Him, sin no more hath dominion
By grace, in his life we may share!

His Word shall not fail you, He promised
He left us his Body and Blood
Here before us dear Jesus is waiting
Men may now eat Angelic Food!

Veni Per Mariam

Antiphon at Vespers, Solemnity of Pentecost
ref. & arr. Jimmy Mitchell (1985-) & Colleen Nixon (1985-)

Come, Holy Spirit
Fill the hearts of Your faithful
Come, Holy Spirit
And enkindle in us the fire of Your love
Send forth Your Spirit, Lord
And we shall be created
And You shall renew the face of the earth

Veni, Sancte Spiritus
Veni per Mariam

O God, who by the light of the Holy Spirit
Did instruct the hearts of Your faithful
Grant that in the same Spirit
We may be truly wise
And ever rejoice in His consolation
Through the same Christ Our Lord

Come, Holy Spirit
Come through Your beloved spouse
Come, Holy Spirit
Come through her Immaculate Heart
Come to me and abide with me
Always and forever

What Wondrous Love

William Walker (1809-1875)
v. 4 Jimmy Mitchell (1985-) © 2011 Mysterium

What wondrous love is this, O my soul, O my soul!
What wondrous love is this, O my soul!
What wondrous love is this that caused the Lord of bliss
To bear the dreadful curse, for my soul, for my soul
To bear the dreadful curse for my soul.

To God and to the Lamb, I will sing, I will sing
To God and to the Lamb, I will sing
To God and to the Lamb who is the great "I Am"
While millions join the theme, I will sing, I will sing
While millions join the theme, I will sing

And when from death I'm free, I'll sing on, I'll sing on
And when from death I'm free, I'll sing on
And when from death I'm free, I'll sing and joyful be
And through eternity, I'll sing on, I'll sing on
And through eternity, I'll sing on

O Holy Spirit come, dwell in me, dwell in me
O Holy Spirit come, dwell in me
O Holy Spirit come, to dwell in hearts yet won
Through Mary's perfect Heart, Spirit come, Spirit Come
Through Mary's perfect Heart, Spirit come

When I Survey

Isaac Watts (1674-1748)

When I survey the wondrous cross
On which the Prince of glory died
My richest gain I count but loss
And pour contempt on all my pride

Forbid it, Lord, that I should boast
Save in the death of Christ my God!
All the vain things that charm me most
I sacrifice them to His blood

See from His head, His hands, His feet
Sorrow and love flow mingled down!
Did e'er such love and sorrow meet
Or thorns compose so rich a crown?

Were the whole realm of nature mine
That were a present far too small
Love so amazing, so divine
Demands my soul, my life, my all

NOTES

NOTES

NOTES

NOTES

NOTES

NOTES

NOTES

NOTES

NOTES

NOTES

NOTES

MYSTERIUM

LOVE GOOD

Mysterium creates products and events alongside institutions and movements within the Church to help young people discover the mystery of God's love. As Love Good's sacred division, our brands include bestselling records from *Marian Grace*, cinematic music and talks from *Jimmy Mitchell*, and nationwide events such as the *Glory Conference*.

Love Good is a movement of culture built upon a very simple idea: that Beauty can change the world. In an era marked by confusion and isolation, we believe Beauty to be the last standing transcendental that can unite generations, evangelize culture with joy, and ultimately lead every human heart to the Truth for which it longs.

Our team consists of full-time staff and missionary apprentices who accompany young people and artists in the work of evangelizing culture. Please consider joining our movement by becoming a patron. Not only will you be on the front lines of discovering the best new music, books, and craft initiatives from across the world, your patronage will help sustain the ongoing efforts of young aspiring saints you can believe in.

Visit **LoveGoodCulture.com** to learn more.

#letsbesaintstogether